THE
MISCELLANY

OF

Sex

TANTALIZING TRAVELS
THROUGH LOVE, LUST
AND LIBIDO

FRANCESCA TWINN

D0124147

Capella

This edition published in 2007 by Arcturus Publishing Limited
26/27 Bickels Yard, 151–153 Bermondsey Street,
London SE1 3HA

In Canada published for Indigo Books
468 King St W,
Suite 500,
Toronto,
Ontario M5V 1L8

ISBN: 978-1-84193-837-0

Printed in China

Art director: Beatriz Waller
Designer: Adelle Morris

CONTENTS

For my parents who made me with love
For Olivia, welcome to the world
And for those on their way...

Heartfelt thank yous to all, especially
to my sexy assistant Danielle Seitz
and to the passionate Matt Chittock,
Cheryl Davison and Terry Wilson for
their suggestive contributions, to Tim
Glynne-Jones and Nigel Matheson
for supportive healing and
encouragement and to all friends for
their helpful flirtations. It's been a
pleasure.

FOREPLAY

While pondering the infinite possibilities of love and libido, it has been hard not to also consider the meaning of life…

Many spend their time looking for that special someone to whisper those three little words to, while others seek pleasure or solace in three big letters – S E X. Is the answer meaningless sex or a meaningful relationship? Or is it a combination of both?

This light-hearted, sometimes serious, candid and hopefully surprising book ventures into comfort and danger zones alike. It is filled with stories and statistics, facts and figures, compelling accounts, moments of madness and comical tales. Since time began, particular ways of behaving, time-honoured traditions and strange fascinations have developed which illustrate how the world views sex. The battle of the sexes has long been a favourite sport of the human race, not to mention the vast and much-explored areas of orientation, position, and imagination. It all proves that, when it comes to the meaning of sex, there is no simple definition.

While love may prove elusive, one thing is for sure – sex is a fact of all our lives. Well, let's face it, we wouldn't be here without it.

Francesca Twinn, Brighton 2007

THIS IS SEX

Welcome to the wonderful and sublime world of sex, represented in so many forms and attitudes, shapes and sizes, desires and orientations, cultures and styles the world over.

S-E-X

Sex may be a simple three-letter word, but it keeps the world spinning day after day. If you google 'sex', you get roughly 425 million entries, which is more than 'god' (365 million), 'president' (359 million) and 'porn' (104 million), but it doesn't beat old-fashioned 'love' (887 million), a term which admittedly covers a multitude of sins. The World Health Organization estimates there are 100 million acts of human sexual intercourse every day, which sounds conservative in a world with a population of 6.6 billion (in 2007), which is increasing by over 200,000 every day. Yes, people like sex.

'We must reckon with the possibility that something in the nature of the sexual instinct itself is unfavourable to the realization of complete satisfaction.' Sigmund Freud, 1912

Cybersex

Studies by Australian psychologists have suggested that Internet porn is the worst culprit for wrecking marriages and that it could be a bigger threat in the future. Reports in 2007 found that, with all types of sexual desires easily catered for online, there has been an increase in men engaging in secret and compulsive activities, which take the place of real intimacy and fuel a sense of inadequacy in their partners. But according to Nielsen/Net Ratings NetView, one in three visitors to adult websites was a woman.

QUIRKY WORD SEARCHES

❖WET AND MESSY SHOES – *this takes you to the high end of women's fashion shoes, for example Prada and Manolo Blahniks, dripping with milk, covered in sand and coated with mud for the pleasure of foot fetishists*

❖JAPANESE AMPUTEE SEX DOLLS – *designed for teratophiliacs and those who can't bear their lover to leave…*

❖NAIL PASSION – *for those who like their cuticles cute and on someone else*

❖SANDALS AND SOCKS – *the chance to send in a personal photograph sitting in your front room in Y-fronts, sandals and socks*

❖CAST FETISH – *a journey into the world of casts and braces, complete with intricate medical histories*

We are not aroused

A 2006 UK relationship survey by arousal oil company Zestra revealed that one in 10 women has sex but doesn't enjoy it. The same number fake orgasms.

Chemistry lesson

In *Anatomy of Love* (1992), anthropology professor Helen Fisher identified three biochemical processes in relationships which shape our reproductive strategies. The first, fuelled by testosterone and oestrogen, gives us our initial sex drive. The second, falling in love and developing attachments, involves dopamine, norepinephrine and phenylethylamine which combine to produce euphoria. The third is a result of oxytocin, vasopressin and serotonin, which give us intimacy, trust and affection. Most people would sum up the three stages as lust, being in love and long-term attachment.

STRANGE WORLD

❇ Karl Watkins, 20, appeared in Hereford Crown Court, England, accused of outraging public decency by making love to pavements. He also tried to 'mount an underpass'. One witness spoke of seeing Watkins' naked buttocks pumping up and down as passers-by gathered. Having served an 18-month sentence, Watkins was back in court charged with simulating sex with black plastic bin bags in front of teenage girls. He said his ultimate fantasy was to be in a dustcart when the bin bags were crushed. ❇ *Dacryphilia is the enjoyment of sexual arousal from seeing tears in the eyes of your partner.* ❇ Japanese porn actress Hitomi Tachikawa was born with two vaginas; she made her film debut in the 1985 thriller *Two to Love.* ❇ *Robert Stewart, a 51-year-old bachelor, is alleged to have been found by cleaners naked from the waist down enjoying an intimate moment with his bicycle at a private hostel in Ayr, Scotland.* ❇ In the 19th century many doctors believed that women need an orgasm to conceive. ❇ *'Underdressing' is the practice of wearing female garments under male clothes: low-budget film-maker Ed Woods liked nothing better than to sport women's underwear beneath his military uniform during World War II.*

IS SHE OR ISN'T HE?

✱ It's unclear whether James Miranda Barry (1795–1865) was the world's first female doctor or not. During Barry's lifetime, he (or she) lived as a man, but after Barry's death pregnancy scars were apparently discovered on

her (or his) body. ✱ *The Chevalier d'Eon lived the first half of his life as a man and the second as a woman. Anatomically, he was male.* ✱ George Sand, the female French novelist, habitually wore male clothing. ✱ *Lord Cornbury (1661–1723), the governor of New Jersey and New York, is said to have received visitors on the Queen's birthday dressed as the Queen herself, which raised an eyebrow or two.* ✱ In 1933, Maurice Wilson announced that he planned to crash-land a plane on the slopes of Everest before walking to the summit and planting a silken Union Jack. He was found dead on the slopes the following year. Curiously, there are rumours that when Wilson was discovered he was wearing women's underwear and had items of women's clothing in his baggage. In 1960 a woman's shoe was found at 21,000 feet on Everest, further fuelling speculation that, when Wilson set out to conquer Everest, he did so as a woman.

The knowledge

A recent survey by the Family Planning Association in the UK has shown people are ignorant on the subject of sex, with a third thinking that a shower, exercise or going to the toilet can prevent pregnancy.

'As a child I was taken to the pantomime or the theatre and I would always, always fall in love with somebody on the stage. And want to have sex with them.' Ewan McGregor

'Your perception is your reality.
Experts say the brain is the biggest sex organ.'
Melinda Hemmelgarn, dietician and broadcaster

MEN AND WOMEN NOW

In 2007, *Sex & the Psyche* revealed a contemporary study of 19,000 British men and women of all orientations. Psychotherapist Brett Kahr found that porn is used by 90 per cent of men and 60 per cent of women, and online porn by 48 per cent of men and 9.5 per cent of women. The language used in answers by a substantial number of the men was less romantic and more pornographic. More men are unfaithful; women are less likely to have an orgasm. Spanking fantasies came from 18 per

cent of men and 7 per cent of women, while 16 per cent of women and 4 per cent of men don't fantasize. Of those that do, 28 per cent of women think about sex with two men, and 58 per cent of men think about bedding two women, while other topics included vampires and aliens. Only 3 per cent of people say they are gay, while 4 per cent are bi and 1 per cent aren't sure.

'Friends with benefits' are members of modern groups of companions who hang out and enjoy sex together with no strings.

♦♦♦

'Dejafuck' is someone a person has had sex with before or, embarrassingly, only remembers during the act.

Quickies

■ Apparently, women talk dirty more than men.

■ A whale penis is called a 'dork'.

■ Women with PhDs are twice as likely to go for anonymous sex as women without a degree.

■ Female *Cosmo*-readers who do the sex surveys have five times more lovers than other women.

■ President Warren Harding is believed to have habitually had sex with a woman 30 years younger in a White House broom cupboard.

■ Twenty per cent of women in couples have more than one sexual partner.

■ Australian women are more likely to have sex on a first date than American women.

■ More college women prefer to have oral sex than dropouts.

■ Women with a positive sexual attitude tend to be lower achievers.

■ Author Ian Fleming thought women, like champagne, were 'there to be drunk'.

■ Casanova dressed as a woman and was a librarian, but he would now be considered anti-feminist.

■ Janenne Swift, an LA secretary, officially married a 50lb rock in 1976.

AVN (Adult Video News) Awards 2007

Best New Starlet: *Naomi* ❖ Female Performer of the Year: *Hillary Scott* ❖ Male Performer of the Year: *Tommy Gunn* ❖ Bestselling Title of the Year: *Pirates*

Are we having sex yet?

According to the Office of National Statistics, one in eight women between the ages of 16 and 50 didn't have any sex in the space of a year and most only had one partner. One in six men under 70 had no sex and only 12 per cent had more than one partner.

HARDCORE OR HARDBOILED

In the Realm Of The Senses (Ai No Corrida, 1976) is a Japanese movie that tells the true story of a couple who get into a bit of bother in 1920s Tokyo, when they lock themselves in a room for a couple of weeks and agree to literally shag themselves to death. One of them anyway, since she is found wandering the streets in a daze, his severed penis in her pocket after a dose of autoerotic asphyxiation. The movie is famous for its real-action sex scenes: the viewer is sitting, watching and thinking, yes, she really does have him in her mouth. For a relatively mainstream film, it remains controversial. But it isn't a hardcore porn film. There's a scene with a boiled egg too.

International affairs

❖The French called syphilis THE ENGLISH MALADY; the English used to call it THE FRENCH DISEASE ❖ A FRENCH LETTER is a condom in English; AN ENGLISH OVERCOAT is a condom in French, or *redingote anglaise* ❖ THE ITALIAN HABIT, meaning anal intercourse, may come from Shakespeare ❖ AN IRISH TOOTHPICK is an erect penis ❖ AN AMERICAN SOCK is East African slang for a condom ❖ RUSSIAN is the word on the street for male masturbation between a woman's breasts ❖ A DUTCH WIFE is a sex doll to the Japanese, just as a TURKISH BATH is slang for a brothel ❖ Across Europe THE ENGLISH VICE has come to mean sado-masochistic activity, especially if it involves a cane or riding crop ❖ UGANDAN AFFAIRS is a term for sexual intercourse invented by UK magazine *Private Eye* after a female journalist explained away a sexual encounter by saying, 'We were upstairs discussing Uganda.'

'Drinking when we are not thirsty and making love all year round; that is all there is to distinguish us from other animals.'
Beaumarchais, *Le Mariage de Figaro*, 1785

'If sex is such a natural phenomenon, how come there are so many books on how to do it?' Bette Midler

HEADLINES

➤ CREATURE THAT HAS NOT HAD SEX FOR 100M YEARS ➤ PANDA MATING FAILS; VETERINARIAN TAKES OVER ➤ NEVER WITHHOLD HERPES FROM LOVED ONE ➤ IS THERE A RING OF DEBRIS AROUND URANUS? ➤ PROSTITUTES APPEAL TO POPE ➤ FIRST-TIME EXOTIC DANCERS SHOULD AVOID THE POLE ➤ LESBIAN JAPANESE MONKEYS CHALLENGE DARWIN'S ASSUMPTIONS ➤ GRANDMOTHER GIVES SEX ADVICE ON OXYGEN ➤ ORGAN FESTIVAL ENDS IN SMASHING CLIMAX ➤ MAN WHIPS FIANCÉE WITH CAT ➤ SOVIET VIRGIN LANDS SHORT OF GOAL AGAIN ➤ QUEEN MARY HAVING BOTTOM SCRAPED ➤ DR RUTH TO TALK ABOUT SEX WITH NEWSPAPER EDITORS

AN A–Z OF TERMS

APHALLATOSIS – *mental disorder resulting from sexual frustration* ♦ BB – *bareback, sex without a condom* ♦ CANADIAN BACON – *uncircumcized penis* ♦ DECORATORS ARE IN, THE – *having a period* ♦ EDDIE GRUNDIES – *British slang for underpants* ♦ FOX HUNTER – *promiscuous heterosexual man* ♦ GAMETOPHOBIA – *fear of marriage* ♦ HAIRY SADDLEBAG – *the scrotum* ♦ IDIOGAMIST – *person who is only sexually responsive to their spouse* ♦ JO-BAG – *a condom* ♦ KETTLEDRUMS – *breasts* ♦ LAGNESIS – *excessive sexual desire* ♦ MACKEREL – *old-fashioned slang for a pimp* ♦ NAMELESS, THE – *reference to the vagina in Victorian times* ♦ OAO – *one and only (or on-and-off) sweetheart* ♦ PASSION FLAPS – *the labia* ♦ QUACK – *an ugly girl or boy, as well as a short, sharp fart* ♦ RR1 – *Rural Route 1, US code for sex with a prostitute* ♦ SKEEZA – *woman who swops sex for cocaine* ♦ TAKE THE FATAL LEAP – *propose marriage* ♦ UTEROMANIA – *insatiable female desire* ♦ VD – *venereal disease* ♦ WOMEN IN COMFORTABLE SHOES – *lesbians* ♦ XENOPHILIA – *attraction to strangers* ♦ YONI – *the vagina or vulva* ♦ ZIPLESS FUCK – *sex without involvement*

WILD WOMEN

Meredith Chivers of the Center for Addiction and Mental Health and J Michael Bailey of Northwestern University exposed 18 heterosexual men and 18 heterosexual women to two films, one of human sex, the other of bonobo monkey sex. The study, published in 2005, found the men were aroused by female humans only, while the women showed signs of arousal from humans (straight and gay) as well as animal copulation. Psychiatry professor Barbara Bartlik was  not surprised and suggested the men may have worried about being labelled homosexual or perverse and were therefore inhibited.

'Love is the answer, but while you are waiting for the answer, sex raises some pretty good questions.' Woody Allen

THE WORLD'S SEXIEST

➤ SCARLETT JOHANSSON: *Glamour* magazine's sexiest body 2007 ➤ JESSICA ALBA: *FHM's* sexiest woman 2007 ➤ TAKE THAT: top of *New Woman's* Sexiest Men in the World 2007. ROBBIE WILLIAMS came in at number 10, while PRINCE HARRY is three places higher than PRINCE WILLIAM. ➤ In 2007, GoVeg.com's World's Sexiest Vegetarians were KEVIN EUBANKS and CARRIE UNDERWOOD taking over from 2006's PRINCE and KRISTIN BELL ➤ BRITISH: Budget Travel Online's sexiest accent 2007 ➤ GEORGE CLOONEY: *People's* sexiest man alive 2006 ➤ MATTHEW MCCONAUGHEY: *People's* Sexiest Man of the Year 2005

Quickies

■ Aztecs mixed eagle poo with calabash tree fruit pulp to use as a contraceptive.

■ In 1980, Majorcan hoteliers claimed that over-enthusiastic honeymooners cost them more than a million dollars a year in damaged beds.

■ Albert Einstein and Charles Darwin both married first cousins.

■ Apparently, having a baby is the second most popular reason to have sex.

■ 18th century prostitutes could avoid penalties if they joined the opera.

■ One billion Valentine's cards are bought each year in the US.

■ The off-limits Elvis Suite in the Playboy Mansion is where the King spent a 1970s night with eight girls.

■ Swinging is rumoured to have been common between US pilots and their wives during the 1950s.

■ Founded in New York, cake parties are events celebrating female sexual equality, full of lingerie and hot women, with men welcome by invitation only.

■ Dreaming of sex literally means the desire for sex. Uninhibited dreams usually mean the dreamer is inhibited when awake.

■ Henry VI banned kissing as he thought it was responsible for disease.

■ Only 4 per cent of men ask their girlfriend's parents for their daughter's hand in marriage.

■ Your heart beats more than 100,000 times a day.

■ A 'drive-thru' is someone known to be easy to get into bed.

■ A survey showed that 56 per cent of people have had sex at work.

'We are at a major epoch in human history, which is that we don't need sex to recreate the race. You can have babies without sex. This is the first time in human history that has been true, and it means, for example, we could do some extraordinary things.'

David Cronenberg, film director

FIRST STIRRINGS

Although scientists don't know about the exact origins of sex or early intimate relationships, they do know humans have been doing it since the beginning of their existence. After all, where on earth would we be without it?

AND ADAM 'KNEW' EVE

❀ Many believe that Original Sin is 'sex', but in the Bible God created man with the intention of procreation: 'Be fruitful and increase in number.'

❀ One day The Lord came to Adam, and said, 'I've got some good news and some bad news.' Adam said, 'Well, give me the good news first.'

The Lord explained, 'I've got two new organs for you. One is called a brain. It will allow you to create new things, solve problems, and have intelligent conversations with Eve. The other organ I have for you is called a penis. It will give you great physical pleasure and allow you to reproduce your now intelligent life form and populate this planet. Eve will be very happy that you now have this organ and can give her children.'

Adam, very excited, exclaimed, 'These are great gifts you have given to me. What could possibly be bad news after such great tidings?'

The Lord looked upon Adam and said with great sorrow, 'You will never be able to use these two gifts at the same time.'

'We have reason to believe that man first walked upright
to free his hands for masturbation.'
Lily Tomlin, actress

First Sex Records

▶ The oldest sex manuals date from about 2,500BC, thanks to Huang-Ti, the Yellow Emperor, and were way ahead of the West's efforts.

▶ The first educational literature on sexual intercourse was written in India. The most ancient texts were the Vedas, in which sex was

a moral ritual of shared pleasure between married couples.

▶ The earliest sex manuscripts, written 2,400 years ago, were found in 1973 in the Chinese tomb of Dai Marquis Licang, the Prime Minister of the King of Changshai from 193BC.

'Where do babies come from? Don't bother asking adults.
They lie like pigs. However, diligent independent research and hours
of playground consultation have yielded fruitful if tentative, results.
There are several theories. Near as we can figure out,
it has something to do with acting ridiculous in the dark.
We believe it is similar to dogs when they act peculiar and ride each
other. This is called "making love". Careful study of popular song
lyrics, advertising catchlines, TV sitcoms, movies and T-shirt
inscriptions offers us significant clues as to its nature.
Apparently, it makes grown-ups insipid and insane. Some graffiti
was once observed that said, "Sex is good". All available evidence,
however, points to the contrary.' Matt Groening, *The Simpsons*

PIECES OF THE PUZZLE

♦ Long before human procreation, life on earth was created by asexual single-celled organisms. Scientists discovered fossilized evidence that sexual reproduction was going strong within one billion years of the planet's formation.

♦ The human body has remained largely unchanged for 100,000 years, while shifting ideas have affected the ways in which people view sex and what they find sexy. Some experts suggest cavemen would have had sex for pleasure and compare the early humans with the bonobo monkey. This creature shares more than 98 per cent of its DNA with humans and enjoys sex with many partners, regardless of age, sex or anything else. However, humans are equally close to the combat-prone chimpanzee, which has sex solely to reproduce. And while bonobos substitute aggression for pleasure, people have evolved choosing to make war as well as love.

♦ Mesopotamia is the source of the earliest records of human history. Women and men celebrated sex in the temple of Ishtar, goddess of love, fertility and sex.

♦ Up until the 17th century, it was commonly believed that God or some early big bang created mankind. Charles Darwin first looked at the peacock and wondered why it would display its plumage, which could attract predators, without a worthwhile reason. His theories on evolution in his book *On the Origin of Species* (1859) introduced the ideas of sexual and natural selection.

♦ Psychologist Susan Blackmore says humans focus on memes, forms of imitation, and that sex, power and food are the most popular subjects.

'Pleasure is the beginning and end of the blessed life.'
Epicurus c. 341–270BC

According to Morris

According to theories put across by zoologist Desmond Morris in his seminal 1967 book *The Naked Ape*, the beginnings of intimacy and emotional commitment in human sexuality came about not long after people started walking upright. This development led to a narrower pelvis, which in turn led to smaller, more dependent offspring that needed care from a united, more family-like unit. Following on from that, Morris asserts, was the rise of sexual selection, which was evolutionarily responsible for some of the features we enjoy today, such as less body hair, erogenous zones, breasts and buttocks and the female orgasm.

The chicken and the egg are lying in bed. The chicken is smoking a cigarette with a satisfied smile on its face, while the egg is frowning and looking decidedly disappointed.
'I guess we answered that question,' mutters the egg.

A POTTED HISTORY OF SEX

The beginning Adam and Eve

1300BC Women were virtuous, free and strong, but gradually lost their influence over men

500BC Socrates on marriage: 'By all means marry; if you get a good wife, you'll become happy, if you get a bad one, you'll become a philosopher'

480–400BC The Greek words *eros* and *agape* – carnal and spiritual – were used to distinguish more than one type of love

400BC Hippocrates, the father of sexual medicine, said a woman's

orgasm stopped at the point sperm entered the womb and her partner's pleasure ceased

320BC Theophrastus promoted satyrion, a plant that, he claimed, helped a man to perform 70 times over

48BC Cleopatra began her affair with Caesar

42BC Cleopatra seduced Mark Antony

AD68 In Rome, asses milk was believed to promote virility when rubbed on the genitals

300 *The Kama Sutra* was written by Vatsyayana

900 The tragic tale of love between Tristan and Isolde first appeared

1057 Lady Godiva made her tax protest, riding naked through Coventry in England
1227 Ulrich von Lichtenstein travelled from Venice to Austria dressed as Venus
1228 Women were allowed to propose, first in Scotland, followed by Europe
1382 The word 'sex' was coined in a translation of the Latin Bible
1611 Mary Frith was the first woman arrested for dressing like a man
1613 Don Juan appeared in *The Joker of Seville*
1631 Eighth wonder of the world the Taj Mahal was built as a symbol of love by Emperor Shah Jahan on the death of his wife
1670 The London Dancing Club opened with rampant exhibitionist shows
1725 Giovanni Giacomo Casanova was born and later named 100 of his lovers in his memoirs
1745 Benjamin Franklin promoted the love of an older woman as she would be 'grateful'
1750 *Fanny Hill* was published
1757 *Covent Garden Ladies first* published – a list of London prostitutes (see p.50)
1777 The Marquis de Sade was arrested for obscene sexual practices in Paris and imprisoned in the Château de Vincennes dungeon

1792 Mary Wollstonecraft's *Rights of Women* signified the birth of emancipation
1836 *A Monk's Awful Disclosures*, a book about nuns and priests having sex by Maria Monk, sold more than 300,000 copies before the Civil War
1839 There were an estimated 933 brothels and 848 houses of ill repute in London
1857 The Obscene Publications Act in England

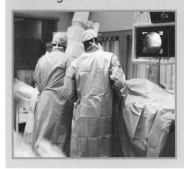

1901 Publication of *Sexual Inversion* by Havelock Ellis
1905 Scientists Nettie Stevens and Edmund Wilson discovered the chromosome determining sex: XX female and XY male
1912 The cure for syphilis was discovered by German Dr Paul Ehrlich
1913 Oral sex was made illegal in the US. Ironically, the 69th piece of legislation was named Act 69
1916 Margaret Sanger opened family planning clinics
1918 Marie Stope's *Married Love* was published
1923 Adultery could now be used as grounds for divorce in England
1936 The first successful amputated penis reconstruction
1944 Ernst Grafenburg first described the G-spot

1946 Pat Riley was the first woman in Australia to wear the bikini and was ordered by police to leave Bondi Beach, Sydney

1948 The Kinsey Report: *Sexual Behavior in the Human Male*

1952 First sex-change operation on US soldier George Jorgensen, who became Christine, performed by Dr Christian Hamburger in Copenhagen, Denmark

1953 Kinsey's *Sexual Behavior in the Human Female* published

1954 William Howell Masters and Virginia Eshelman Johnson began their partnership in sex research and therapy

1957 The London Rubber Company produced Durex, the first lubricated condom

1960 The FDA approved Enovid, the Pill, in the US

1961 The Pill was introduced to Britain as Conovid

1968 First inter-racial kiss on TV between Captain Kirk and Lieutenant Uhura

1972 *The Joy of Sex* was published

1973 Johnny Crawford appeared as the first male full-frontal nude in *Playboy's* September issue

1975 First condom ad in the US with 30 seconds for Trojan. First same-sex marriage in Colorado, which found it had no law preventing the union

1978 Louise Brown was first test-tube baby born in Oldham General Hospital, England

1981 AIDS arrived and a new awareness began

1984 Miss Piggy married Kermit the Frog

1990 Norplant, birth control implants, arrived in the US

1998 FDA approved Viagra for sale

2003 Non-Procreative Sex Act in the US, June 25

LIKE A VIRGIN

... touched for the very first time. Virginity – some lose it, others prefer to hold on to their ha'penny.

> *'Gather ye rosebuds while ye may,*
> *Old time is still a-flying*
> *And this same flower that smiles today,*
> *Tomorrow will be dying.'*

Robert Herrick (1591–1674), *To the Virgins, Make Much of Time*

Cherry Boys

About a quarter of Japanese men aged 30 to 34 are virgins, according to a recent study by the National Institute of Population and Social Security. However, the figure could be even higher as Japan's Cherry Boy Association has reported that many men are too shy or ashamed to reveal their true status, with 11 per cent giving an invalid answer. The 517 members, many of whom hope to meet women and 'graduate' from the club, gather to discuss their virginity and also to hold parties.

WANTON VIRGIN GODDESS

When not at war, Math, the uncle of Welsh goddess Arianrhod, could only survive with his feet resting in the lap of a virgin. Arianrhod's brother Gwydion suggested she could help in this department since she was still chaste. To test her purity, she first had to step over Math's magic rod, but her wanton ways were discovered as, the moment she did so, she gave birth to a boy and a blob, revealing the truth. Although the blob grew into a boy, she took out her anger on him and denied him a name, arms and a wife.

'I knew Doris Day before she was a virgin.' Oscar Levant

NO ENTRY

The chastity belt is from the 19th century and not the Middle Ages as is commonly supposed. In Italy it was called a 'Florentine Girdle'. It wasn't because husbands didn't trust their wives, it was that they didn't trust other men with their wives, so it became a sign of fidelity. Modern belts are sometimes used in BDSM (bondage and S&M). They're made from leather or plastic and can be fastened by padlocks and zips.

---

11 people famous for being virgins

Elizabeth I • Sir Isaac Newton • Immanuel Kant • Mother Teresa • Louis XVI • Havelock Ellis • George Bernard Shaw • Mary, Mother of Jesus • Joan of Arc • Brooke Shields • Britney Spears

---

Vestal Virgins

In ancient Rome, these girls were sworn to celibacy and it was a heinous crime to interfere with them since they were regarded as sacred. This also meant they were buried alive if found to have broken their vow.

'It is one of the superstitions of the human mind to have imagined that virginity could be a virtue.' Voltaire, c. 1735

✳

'What men desire is a virgin who is a whore.'
Edward Dahlberg, *Reasons of the Heart*, 1965

'So a maiden, while she remains untouched, remains dear to her own; but when she has lost her chaste flower with sullied body, she remains neither lovely to boys nor dear to girls.' Catullus (84–54BC)

VIRGIN TRIVIA

✻ The lily was the symbol of virtue and purity in ancient Greece.

✻ In 2007, the US National Center for Health Statistics found that 4 per cent of American adults may be virgins, but 20 per cent have tried hard drugs.

✻ Rosie Reid, 18, decided to auction her virginity on eBay to supplement her income as a student at Bristol University, Englannd. She said she would rather sleep with a stranger than endure three years of poverty. She received more than 400 offers in three days, including one of £10,000.

✻ June is the month most Americans lose their virginity.

✻ Until 1998 deflowered German virgins could claim compensation if the relationship ended.

✻ Women who lose their virginity before the age of 18 are likely to have twice as much sex over a lifetime as those who wait.

✻ A recent study of different nations revealed Austrians are the first to lose their virginity at an average age of 17.3 years, while Malaysians are the last at 23.

✻ In recent years, surgeons in Paris have been doing a roaring trade in hymenoplasties (see p.30) for North African women who wish to become virgins again before they marry or re-marry.

'Where do you put the penis?' The 40 Year Old Virgin (2005)

Immaculate concept

Richard Branson founded Virgin Records in 1972. The name was the suggestion of a colleague who said they were all business virgins. The original logo of naked mirror-image twin girls on top of a huge serpent was designed by Roger Dean.

Father of the Bride

Purity Balls are all the rage in America, with girls promising relieved fathers they are saving themselves for their husbands. In a ceremony celebrating the bond between daughter and dad, vows and rings are exchanged, a covenant of chastity is signed and – not only that – dad also has to promise he will be faithful to mom all over again and not use porn. Virginity pledges are popular among teens, who refrain from sexual intercourse, although research has found this doesn't include other types of sexual activity and that many are not using protection.

VIRGIN FILMS

The Virgin Soldiers (1969) ❖ *The Virgin Suicides* (1999) ❖ *Virgin School* (2007) ❖ *The Virgin Queen* (2005) ❖ *The Last American Virgin* (1982) ❖ *The Virgin and the Gypsy* (1970) ❖ *American Virgin* (2000) ❖ *The Glass Virgin* (1995) ❖ *Virgin Forest* (1985) ❖ *The Married Virgin* (1918) ❖ *Mary Jane's Not a Virgin Anymore* (1997) ❖ *Virgin High* (1991) ❖ *Virgin Territory* (2007) ❖ *Attack of the Virgin Mummies* (2004) ❖ *The Foolish Virgin* (1924) ❖ *Virgin Beasts* (2005) ❖ *Virgin Larry* (2000) ❖ *The Virgin of Liverpool* (2003) ❖ *A Virgin Paradise* (1921) ❖ *Virgin Sacrifice* (1959) ❖ *The Wise Virgin* (1924)

Slang for Losing It

Blaze the trail ❦ break in the balls ❦ break the teacup ❦ bury the hobbit ❦ cherry harvest ❦ coitus acceptus ❦ crack the pipkin ❦ cut the cake ❦ deflower ❦ has-been ❦ lost honour ❦ pick-a-lock ❦ pop the cherry ❦ pluck a rose ❦ ruin the rug ❦ Turkish delight

'The tragedy of sexual intercourse is the perpetual virginity of the soul.' William B Yeats

THE FIRST TIME

*'In their first affairs women are in love with their lovers,
later they are in love with love.'* La Rochefoucauld

✳

*'She thought that I knew/and I thought that she knew/so both of us
were willing, but we didn't know how to do it.'*
Elvis Costello, 'Mystery Dance', 1977

Lost Age

A third of people were aged below 16 when they lost their virginity, according to a worldwide survey by Durex in 2005, with Icelandic teens the youngest and Indians the oldest at an average of 19.8 years old. Results showed that the age keeps decreasing.

SECOND TIME AROUND

Hymenoplasty is surgery for women who want to return to a virginal state and have their first time all over again. One 40-year-old woman from San Antonio in the US had the operation done as a gift to her husband to celebrate their wedding anniversary. Apparently the reconstruction can cost about $3,500, and can be carried out in day surgeries in America, Japan and western Europe, but is banned in some other countries.

'I remember the first time I had sex – I kept the receipt.'
Groucho Marx

✳

'I want to wait to have sex until I'm married.' Britney Spears

'I had to lie so much about sex, first when I was 15, because I wasn't supposed to be having it. And then when I got older, I lied to everybody I was having sex with, so I could have sex with other people.' Cybill Shepherd

---

FAMOUS FIRST CLAIMS

50 CENT: **12**, with a woman in her 20s ★ KIRK DOUGLAS: **15**, with a teacher in 1932 ★ MARIAH CAREY: **23**, on her wedding night ★ BILLY IDOL: **11**, to the original version of 'Mony Mony' ★ LISA KUDROW: **31**, on her wedding night ★ SEAN CONNERY: **8**... ★ IGGY POP: **20** ★ JOHN HOLMES: **12**, to his friend's 36-year-old mother ★ GENE SIMMONS: **13**, during a paper round ★ COLIN FARRELL: **15**, with an Australian woman 20 years older that he met at a gay club ★ JERRY HALL: **14**, with a rodeo bull rider ★ DUSTIN HOFFMAN: **15**, in the dark with a woman who thought she was with his brother ★ BROOKE SHIELDS: with Superman – at university with Dean Cain ★ JERRY SPRINGER: **17**, for $10 with a New Orleans hooker

---

'A little still she strove, and much repented, and whispering, "I will ne'er consent" – consented.' Lord Byron

Single mothers

Figures from the National Center for Health Statistics in the US showed a rise in pregnancies of single mothers, more than half in their 20s, with 1.5 million births in 2004. The $50m Abstinence Education Program from the Department of Health and Human Services suggested that women abstain from sex until their 30s.

FERTILITY

Lovestruck

St Valentine's Day, named after an early Christian martyr, almost certainly has its origins in the Graeco-Roman holidays devoted to fertility and love such as the *Lupercalia* (the feast of Lupercus, the wolf hunter) on the 14th and 15th February, of which Plutarch wrote: 'At this time many of the noble youths and of the magistrates run up and down through the city naked, for sport and laughter striking those they meet with shaggy thongs. And many women of rank get in their way deliberately, and like children at school present their hands to be struck, believing that the pregnant will thus be helped in delivery and the barren to pregnancy.'

✳ **May Day** *The holiday around 1 May has been observed since ancient Gaelic and Celtic times in honour of Bel, the Celtic god of light, fire and sun. Bonfires marked purification while leaping over flames was said to increase fertility. Celebrants also danced around a phallic maypole and enjoyed sexual activity in the woods.*

✳ **The Easter Bunny** *Hiding chocolate eggs for children wasn't really the point of the original mythical rabbit. As one of nature's fast breeders, it was an obvious*

symbol of fertility, but, when the pagan goddess Eostre saved a bird which turned into a rabbit that still laid eggs, it became the Easter Bunny, aka the Spring Bunny in the US.

✳ **Stonehenge** *Among numerous explanations given for the ancient*

English site in Wiltshire, a researcher from the University of British Columbia suggested in 2003 that it is actually making a big statement on fertility. Apparently, the shape of the stones resembles the female sexual organ, the opening of Mother Earth.

* **The rite stuff** *During the Neolithic period the finger and ring symbolized the phallus and the vulva, signifying the earth goddess*

and the underworld god during sexual intercourse.
• At Cantonese funerals, daughters-in-law cover their abdomens in green cloth – symbolizing rebirth/fertility – and rub themselves against coffins to extract the last vestiges of life from the dead. • *In ancient Europe, women drank a potion made of powdered hare's womb, sparrow's brain or wolf's penis to increase fertility; to decrease it, they swore by the teeth and fingers of a dead child, or the testicles of a weasel.* • Women who want to conceive sleep on the 27-foot-long erect penis of the Cerne Abbas Giant, a 180-foot figure carved in chalk in the Dorset hills.

HOUNEN MATSURI

This Japanese fertility festival is celebrated at the Tagata Jinja shrine in Komaki. Often called the 'penis shrine', it is about 1,500 years old. It stands next to a building called the *Shinmeisha* which is packed with penis-shaped objects, some of which are natural and some of which are man-made. The phallus represents the power of nature to renew itself. Every year on 15 March, a new two-and-a-half-metre phallus, carved from a cypress tree, is paraded from the Kumoano shrine to the Tagata, where the old phallus is replaced and then sold.

PLAYTIME

GOOD VIBRATIONS

The first electro-mechanical vibrators appeared in the late 19th century. Hand-cranked, they were sold as 'medical instruments'. The idea put across was that they treated 'hysteria' in women by vulvular massage, leading to 'hysterical paroxysm' (aka an orgasm). Portable mains-operated electric vibrators became available in 1902, but erotic films of the 1920s gave the game away, exposing their true purpose as sex aids. Today, rabbit vibrators – dildos with 'bunny ears' which sit on either side of the clitoris – have twitched their way to the world's number one sex toy. Rampant Rabbit, Pearl Rabbit (seen in *Sex and The City*) and Jessica Rabbit are trade names. Nothing stays still in the world of vibrators and 49-year-old housewife Joanne Dryesdale of Utah invented the Vortex Vibrator after enjoying the sensation of air on her fingertips when unblocking the nozzle of her vacuum cleaner. She claims her vibrator, which attaches to domestic cleaning devices, can bring a woman to climax in 10 seconds.

NOVELTY TOYS

The zero-gravity sex chair ❖ mobile-phone-radiation-proof underwear for men ❖ a vibrator extension that plugs into an electric toothbrush ❖ Japanese silk bondage ropes ❖ remote-controlled vibrators ❖ hands-free 'butterflies'

German footballers Michael Ballack and Oliver Kahn successfully sued sex shop Beate Uhse for €50,000 for marketing vibrators under the names 'Michael B.' and 'Olli K.'.

ANCIENT SEX AIDS

Artificial sex organs shaped from carved-out pumpkins or bamboo moistened with oil ✱ *dolls* ✱ *devices mentioned in the* Kama Sutra *included dildos made of gold, silver, wood, rubber or horn* ✱ *stone dildos, anal toys and ring-shaped devices featured in an ancient 'sex shop' unearthed in Peru* ✱ *Chinese dildos made of jade or bronze* ✱ *the soft touch preferred by the Greeks of a faux phallus made of padded leather softened with oil* ✱ *the ancient Roman selection included dildos made of glass.*

Rubbing them up the wrong way

Sex toys are banned in India. However, in 2007, a new condom caused a bit of a buzz in the country when it was discovered that it vibrates. The ring attachment, said to give pleasure to both parties, led to an outcry from Hindu nationalists who claimed the item was a sex aid in disguise. Contraception is promoted in India to help family planning, population control and to prevent the spread of AIDS.

Box of tricks

In Alabama, state law prevents you buying a sex toy on Valentine's Day. ♦ At least one in five adults around the world has used a vibrator. ♦ The sex-toy industry in the US is worth $8–12 billion annually. ♦ Japanese sex toys often appear in abstract or imaginative designs due to an old law that forbade too close a resemblance to genitalia. ♦ In May 2007, an English village believed it was under attack from terrorists when the bomb squad was called in to blow up a buzzing package. It was a vibrator and a bag of chocolate buttons. ♦ The sex-toy industry has joined the eco-bandwagon through the manufacture of such products as vegan condoms and lubricants, and solar-powered vibrators.

ORGIES

The Greeks

The word 'orgy' originates from the ancient Greek for religious service and referred to rituals in tribute to Dionysus, the god whose remit included wine, ecstasy and madness. His Roman equivalent was Bacchus. Before orgies, the ancient Greeks necked gallons of wine, banging drums, blowing reed pipes and calling out to the gods in the voices of animals. The orgy began when participants became ecstatic, copulating on the ground in a bid to improve the fertility of the soil.

ORGY OF FACTS

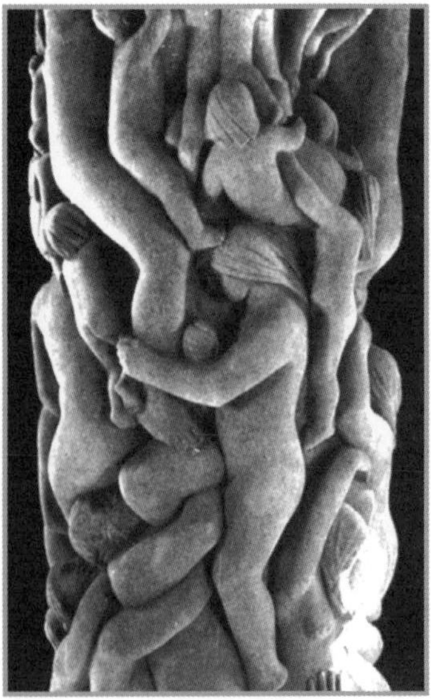

✻ The ancient Slavs held orgies to mark the summer solstice, bathing naked in the rivers to wash away evil, then indulging in group sex. Luckily, it was a 'special night' when sex was not considered sinful. ✻ *In the 13th century in Lithuania, Grand Duke Vytenis ordered his three wives to strip and be 'pleasured by hill-goats' while he and his court observed.* ✻ When animators got bored working on the Walt Disney animation *Snow White* in the 1930s, they put together an explicit orgy scene featuring Snow White and her seven diminutive friends, much to the consternation of Disney who burnt the footage. ✻ *In 2007 Dutch police and park rangers admitted there was little they could do to stop outdoor orgies. In one case, a large group of naked people was spotted in the Bussloo area, including ten couples being 'particularly boisterous' while the others watched.* ✻ Leszek Szwerowski, a 61-year-old pensioner, is suing the makers of a DVD who had promised to pixellate his face in post-production after he had taken part in an orgy with three women who were trying to break the record for having sex with as many men as possible. Szwerowski was highly embarrassed when his nephew saw a DVD, with his uncle clearly shown waiting in line for his turn. ✻ *In 2007, the Royal College of Nursing reported a new craze among London school kids, known as 'daisy chaining'. This involves group sex among*

boys and girls in each other's homes before their parents get home from work. ✻ Justice Antonin Scalia, a friend of George Bush and shooting buddy of Dick Cheney, astonished an audience at Harvard University when he said, 'I even take the position that sexual orgies eliminate social tensions and ought to be encouraged!'

'Home is heaven and orgies are vile.
But you need an orgy, once in a while.' Ogden Nash

ROMAN EMPERORS

Brave and depraved, adventurous and immoral, admired and notorious. Restrained? Not likely. Promiscuous? Absolutely. When it came to sex, the Romans really seized the day.

◆AD14–37 **TIBERIUS**
Spent the last years of his life on the island of Capri; his bedroom walls depicted sexual acts and positions, while he indulged in twisted pleasures with his collection of boys and girls, according to the writer Suetonius anyway, who also accused him of sado-masochism. It is said he particularly enjoyed boys nibbling his genitals in the swimming pool.

◆AD37–41 **GAIUS**
Better known as the insane or cunning hedonist Caligula, depending on accounts. His short four-year reign was packed with incestuous acts with his three sisters. He also engaged in sexual activities with men, auctioned off the services of senators' wives at orgies and liked to order them into his bedroom for private sex sessions, later boasting about what he had done within earshot of their husbands. He seldom held back. Among other acts of lunacy,

he opened a brothel in his palace, appointed his horse to the Senate and declared himself a living god.

◆AD41–54 **CLAUDIUS**
Claudius loved women and, unusually, did not engage sexually with men. He was married four times to 'bad' women; his third wife Messalina, a raving nymphomaniac, took up the challenge of an all-night sex competition with the prostitute Scylla, who gave up at 25 men, while Messalina carried on until the next morning, victorious if not fully satisfied.

◆AD54–68 **NERO**
Said to have been seduced by his mother Agrippina whom he later had murdered. He had two gay marriages as 'wife' to Pythagoras and 'husband' to Sporus, whom he later had castrated. He also married, then murdered, his friend's Otho's wife, Poppaea.

◆AD81–96 **DOMITIAN**
A scandalous womanizer, his first wife Domitia Longina is said to

have joined him in his conquests. He executed three Vestal Virgins and buried the Chief Vestal alive. He kept women for pleasure and is said to have depilated them himself. He also lusted after his niece, forced her to have an abortion, caused her death and then had her deified.

◆ AD180–192 **COMMODUS**

Lazy and morally corrupt, he is believed to have kept a harem of 300 girls and 300 boys and liked to host orgies. He also favoured dressing like the god Hercules and had all the months of the year named after him.

◆ AD218–222 **ELAGABALUS**

Became ruler at 14 and within four years the transvestite emperor had three wives, one a Vestal Virgin – in Roman law, they were sentenced to be buried alive if they broke their chastity vows. He also 'married' his chariot driver, a blond slave called Hierocles, dressed up in his wives' clothing and enjoyed being beaten. Expansively promiscuous, he spent time in brothels playing the part of a prostitute, was partial to large sexual organs and had the well-endowed brought to him for his pleasure. He is also thought to have instructed physicians to create a vagina in his body. One writer of the time, Dio, described Elagabalus standing nude by one of the windows in his palace, cooing at passers-by like a harlot and trying to entice them in. He also wore far too much make-up.

BATTLE OF THE SEXES

ON DIFFERENT PLANETS

Pop psychologist John Gray studied the attitudes of thousands of men, women and couples and came up with the bestselling *Men are from Mars, Women are from Venus* (1992), basically saying that men and women are different: men feel motivated and empowered when they feel 'needed'; women feel motivated and empowered when they feel 'cherished'. Gray's theory is everyone has the same 12 'love needs', but men prioritize one set of six, while women prioritize the other half-dozen.

	Women	Men
1	CARING	TRUST
2	UNDERSTANDING	ACCEPTANCE
3	RESPECT	APPRECIATION
4	DEVOTION	ADMIRATION
5	VALIDATION	APPROVAL
6	REASSURANCE	ENCOURAGEMENT

A man finds a bottle by the sea. He pulls the cork and out pops a genie. 'Thank you for freeing me. In return I will grant you three wishes.' The man is ecstatic, 'First, I want one billion dollars in a Swiss bank account.' Boom! A flash of light and a piece of paper with account numbers appears in his hand. He continues, 'Next, I want a brand-new red Ferrari right here.' Poof! A flash of light and a brand-new shiny red Ferrari appears next to him. 'Finally, I want to be irresistible to women.' Boom! A flash of light. He turns into a box of chocolates.

HE SAID… SHE SAID

'No one will ever win the
battle of the sexes;
there's too much fraternizing
with the enemy.'
Henry Kissinger

✸

'A king is always a king – and a
woman always a woman:
his authority and her sex ever
stand between them and
rational converse.'
Mary Wollstonecraft Shelley

✸

'The desire of the man is for
the woman.
But the desire of the woman is
for the desire of the man.'
Madame de Staël

✸

'The war between the sexes is
the only one in which both sides
regularly sleep with the enemy.'
Quentin Crisp

Mrs Allonby: 'Define us as a sex.'
Lord Illingworth: 'Sphinxes
without secrets…'
Oscar Wilde, *A Woman of No
Importance*, 1894

✸

'Women need a reason to have
sex. Men just need a place.'
Billy Crystal

✸

'The first symptom of love in a
young man is shyness;
the first symptom in a woman,
it's boldness.'
Victor Hugo

And the winner is…

A recent study in Canada using thermal imaging found that women become sexually aroused as quickly as men. Research where women and men watched pornography showed both sexes reached their peak in about 10 minutes.

GOT IT COVERED

'There was an old woman who lived in a shoe, she had so many children she didn't know what to do... Obviously.'

Barry Cryer, *I'm Sorry, I Haven't a Clue*, BBC radio quiz, 1979

Forms of Contraception

Pill ✳ condom ✳ female condom ✳ sponge ✳ cervical cap ✳ Lea's shield ✳ diaphragm ✳ womb veil ✳ lambskin condoms ✳ hormonal implant ✳ SILCS diaphragm is being developed ✳ Invisible Condom made of hardening gel is being developed in Canada's Université Laval, Quebec ✳ abstinence ✳ celibacy

---

'Protestant women may take the pill. Roman Catholic women must keep taking the tablet.' Irene Thomas, broadcaster and writer

PACK OF NINE

♦ *Vagina comes from the Latin for 'sheath'* ♦ *In Japan, condoms have traditionally been available in leather, tortoiseshell and horn* ♦ *Witch hunts were used by the Church to stamp out the teaching of birth control* ♦ *Rumoured historic alternatives include:* ASIA: *oiled paper as a cervical cap;* EUROPE: *beeswax; and* EGYPT: *acidic pessary with honey* ♦ *Casanova called the sheath the 'English overcoat' and experimented using half a lemon as a cap* ♦ *Sheik Condoms displayed a silhouette of Rudolph Valentino* ♦ *The oldest condoms found were from 1640 at Dudley Castle, England* ♦ *The Durex 2005 Global Survey found about 47 per cent of adults worldwide have had unprotected sex with no knowledge of their partner's sexual history* ♦ *The word 'condom' may have come from a Dr Condom or Conton who kept up a constant supply of sheaths to King Charles II.*

BIRTH CONTROL'S HISTORY

Genesis: Withdrawal, coitus interruptus, mentioned in the Bible

1000BC: First sheath is made of linen and used in ancient Egypt

384–322BC: Aristotle is believed to have suggested cedar oil, lead ointment and frankincense oil as spermicides

AD100–200: Cave paintings in Les Combarelles, France suggest use of condoms in Europe

1564: First literary reference to a linen sheath by Gabriele Fallopius of Italy in *De Morbo Gallico Liber Absolutissimus*

1700s: Condoms from animal gut popular in London

1827: Scientists discover the female egg (ovum)

1838: German doctor Friedrich Wilde introduces the Wilde Cap, precursor to the diaphragm

1839: In the US, Charles Goodyear devises vulcanized rubber to

mass-produce condoms

1861: The *New York Times* prints the first condom ad for Dr Power's French Preventatives

1873: The Comstock Law prevents contraception being advertised or sent through the post in the US

1875: Scientific breakthrough proves life is made through the union of sperm and egg

1880: German doctor Wilhelm Mensinga invents the diaphragm, aka the 'cap'

1912: German Julius Fromm develops no-seam condoms. Fromm's Act is first brand

1914: Margaret Sanger is indicted in the US for advising women on the best times for avoiding pregnancy in *The Woman Rebel*

1916: Charges are dropped and Sanger, her sister and friend open the first US birth control clinic in New York

1923: Sanger opens the first legal birth control clinic in the US

1920s: Japanese scientists invent the rhythm method

1926: First pregnancy test

1929: Durex trademark registered. It stands for durability, reliability and excellence

1930: Roman Catholic Church states birth control is a sin

1936: Doctor John Rock opens a rhythm method clinic in Boston

1950s: About $2 million a year is spent on contraception in America

1951: Pope Pius XII approves the rhythm method

1957: Durex launches the first lubricated condom in the UK

1960: Doctors Pincus and John Rock's Enovid is FDA-approved as a birth control pill

1961: The Pill comes to the UK, for married women only at first

1965: In the US, 6.5 million women take the Pill

1968: Despite recommendations of the Papal commission, Pope Paul VI condemns any form of birth control except the rhythm method and abstinence

1980s: With HIV and AIDS, the use of condoms goes up dramatically

1984: About 75 million women take the Pill worldwide

1990s: Flavoured condoms introduced, sizes recognized

2003: On 19 June, the world's largest condom at 300ft went on display at Chennai in India to promote AIDS awareness

---

Condom Nicknames

Johnnies ♦ rubbers ♦ French letters ♦ Mr Prevention ♦ tour guide ♦ prophylactics ♦ love socks ♦ dobbers ♦ salami sling ♦ the goalie ♦ hats ♦ raincoats ♦ gentleman's jerkins ♦ Condomus Maximus ♦ nodding sock ♦ dinger ♦ snake charmer ♦ Bob…

SWINGING

Sex in suburbia

'Key' parties, popular in the 1970s, took place at the home of players, often married couples – hence the term 'wife-swapping' – where male guests placed their keys in a bowl and female players would randomly choose a set and have sex with the owner. 'Swinging' is a term used for likeminded people who meet in private homes or clubs, where they have the freedom to watch and take part in sexual activity with other consenting adults. The Sexual Freedom League, which began in 1963 in New York City and then California, was originally founded by Jefferson Poland to help set up other groups to promote sexual activity and reform, while 'nude parties', which were really orgy events, began when the league was briefly taken over by Richard Thorne in 1966, splitting the league into different groups with varying sexual objectives. These included the Horny Men's and Wanton Women's circles.

SWING SPEAK

CAN ENTERTAIN: *willing to invite people home for swinging* ✦ CAN TRAVEL: *willing to go to someone's home* ✦ CLOSED SWINGING: *separate rooms to avoid married couples seeing each other with someone else* ✦ CULTURE: *fetishisms* ✦ DOCILE: *a willing participant in domination and bondage* ✦ DOMESTIC TRAINING: *household chores in a humiliating fashion* ✦ ENGLISH CULTURE: *spanking or caning* ✦ EXHIBITIONISM: *sex with an audience* ✦ FRENCH CULTURE: *oral sex* ✦ FULL SWAP: *full intercourse with someone other than a partner* ✦ GROUP: *multiple partners* ✦ INDOOR SPORTS: *swinging* ✦ MORESOMES: *more than a threesome* ✦ OPEN DOOR: *couples with other couples* ✦ PARTY CLOTHES: *from lingerie to togas* ✦ ROMAN CULTURE: *orgies* ✦ SOFT: *intimacy via kissing, touching and oral sex* ✦ SWEDISH CULTURE: *hands-on, especially massage* ✦ TICKET: *usually a woman so the man is allowed entrance*

LANGUAGE OF LOVE?

*'I am happy now that George calls on my bedchamber less
frequently than of old. As it is, I now endure but two calls a week,
and when I hear his steps outside my door I lie down on my bed,
close my eyes, open my legs and think of England.'*
Lady Alice Hillingdon's journal, England 1912

MAKING THE BEAST WITH TWO BACKS

There's no shortage of descriptive terms for sex; the one above is used in *Othello* by William Shakespeare. Here are a few more:

A bit of the old in and out ✦ *baking cookies* ✦ *bang* ✦ *bash the beaver* ✦ *bonk* ✦ *bumpin' fuzzies* ✦ *butter the muffin* ✦ *churning butter* ✦ *corrupt the dumplings* ✦ *creamin'* ✦ *dip your wick* ✦ *do the chores* ✦ *drilling the ditch* ✦ *eat cauliflower* ✦ *filling the cream donut* ✦ *five knuckle shuffle* ✦ *front door action* ✦ *get Jack in the orchard* ✦ *growling at the badger* ✦ *hiding the salami* ✦ *hot dog in a jungle* ✦ *laying pipe* ✦ *getting your leg over* ✦ *making ends meet* ✦ *mix your peanut butter* ✦ *the nasty* ✦ *nookie* ✦ *parallel parking* ✦ *pass the gravy* ✦ *pot the pink* ✦ *putting sour cream in the burrito* ✦ *ride the baloney pony* ✦ *rock the casbah* ✦ *roll in the hay* ✦ *saucing the clam* ✦ *shag* ✦ *shooting the goodness* ✦ *shoot the moon* ✦ *storm the trenches* ✦ *taking the old one-eye to the optometrist* ✦ *train through the tunnel* ✦ *the ugly* ✦ *visit the Netherlands* ✦ *walk the dog* ✦ *work the hairy oracle* ✦ *yodel in the valley* ✦ *zallywhacking*

Hanky panky

First recorded in *Punch* in 1841. Thought to derive from the trickery beneath magicians' handkerchiefs and the phrase 'hocus-pocus' used at fairs and carnivals from the 17th century onwards. Became known as improper sexual activity in inappropriate situations, then used, for example, on signs at swimming pools: 'No hanky panky allowed!'

'Bridegroom, dear to my heart, goodly is your beauty, honeysweet' is the first line of what is thought to be the world's oldest love poem. The risqué, sexy Sumerian ballad is about a priestess in love with a king more than 4,000 years ago.

♦♦♦

William Dunbar is also credited with literature's first use of 'c**t', the profanity often found more offensive than 'fuck', featuring in the early-16th-century Scottish verses *The Flyting of Dunbar and Kennedie* as 'c**tbittin' (afflicted with VD).

A bit of how's your father?

Many joke that in Victorian times overprotective fathers hid under their daughters' voluminous skirts at parties to ward off undesirable visitors. Knowing suitors would ask, 'How is your father?' and the reply would let them know if the coast was clear. However, the phrase really comes from 1930s Scottish music hall and movie comedian Harry Tate, who used it as an excuse to change the subject or in place of something he couldn't say.

MAKING WHOOPEE

Thought to be one of many puns from the great phrasemaker of 1920s New York, Walter Winchell, the controversial newspaper columnist and radio personality. It was then used in the title song to the 1928 Broadway comedy musical about love, *Whoopee!*

'Another bride, Another June
Another sunny honeymoon
Another season, Another reason
For makin' whoopee.'
Gus Kahn, 'Making Whoopee', 1928

> *'French is the language that turns dirt into romance.'*
> Stephen King

Dirty talk is often used to spice up sex: compliments, innuendo, fantasies, what you want to do to your partner and what you want done to you. And pillow talk generally takes place after sex. This all sounds better in French. France has long been associated with

romance, much of it oozing from Paris, the city of love and desire, with an accent many swoon to, plus a history of decadence, eroticism and risqué entertainment. French language literature first became known as 'romance' during Anglo-Norman times, with tales of chivalry, great deeds and romance, typically set at King Arthur's court. The strange thing is its magic still works.

VERBAL GAFFES ON TV

'What does it feel like being rammed up the backside by Barrichello?' James Allen in an interview with Ralf Schumacher

✱

'She was practising fastest finger first by herself in bed last night.'
Who Wants To Be A Millionaire? host Chris Tarrant about the first UK winner
Judith Keppel

✱

'And this is Gregoriava from Bulgaria. I saw her snatch this morning and it was amazing!' Weightlifting commentator Pat Glenn

✱

'One of the reasons Arnie [Arnold Palmer] is playing so well is that before each tee shot, his wife takes out his balls and kisses them. Oh my God! What have I just said?' US PGA commentator

The F-word

The most famous four-letter word in the English language, ultimately meaning 'sexual intercourse', looks very much like its cognates in the Germanic languages, such as *ficken*, the Middle Dutch *focken*, Norwegian dialect *fukka* and Swedish dialect *focka*. Etymologist Eric Partridge associated it with the Indo-European root *peuk*, meaning 'to prick', 'pounce', 'punctuate' and 'point', and also the Latin word *future*, 'to copulate'. However, according to the *Oxford English Dictionary (OED)* and other sources, these links are uncertain. Suggestions of possible Anglo-Saxon origins include a charter from AD772 featuring the place name of 'Fuccerham', which could be the home of the 'fucker', man or beast, possibly famed for doing just that; plus a number of acronyms, including 'Fornicate Under Command of the King' and 'Forced Unlawful Carnal Knowledge', but these are all considered unlikely. 'Fuck' is believed to have entered the English language around the 15th century. It was first written in a satirical poem about the Carmelite friars of Cambridge, *Flen, Flyss* (c1500), where it makes an appearance in humorous Latin code: '*Non sunt in coeli, quia gxddbov xxkxzt pg ifmk*', broken into '*Non sunt in coeli, quia fvccant vvivys of helo*', which translates as 'They are not in heaven because they fuck wives of Ely'. The *OED* cites the work of Scottish poet William Dunbar, *Brash of Wowing*, 1503, as the first 'fuck' in print, with 'Be his feiris he wald haue fukkit'. By the 18th century, 'fuck' was considered an obscenity and no longer tolerated; it was banned from the *OED* until 1972. In 1960, US company Grove Press won the right to sanction 'fuck's' first legal use in print in *Lady Chatterley's Lover*, also appearing three years later in the UK. In 1965, writer Kenneth Tynan was the first person to say it on British TV during a live debate on the BBC, causing an outcry. Still recognized as shocking and vulgar today, the F-word has managed to increasingly saturate our lives, from the schoolyard to television chefs, and despite its sexual connotations, it is generally used to accentuate expressions.

SEX IN VICTORIAN ENGLAND

There's an enduring myth that the Victorians' inhibitions about sex were so extreme that they actually covered up piano legs to discourage any association with the female ankle, but the truth is the Victorians had a powerful, if repressed, sexual appetite. After all, this was a time when prostitution was legal and the perusal of erotica was many a gentleman's discreet pastime and pleasure.

On the game

In 1841, when London had a population of two million, the Police Department put the number of prostitutes at 7,000, but the Society for the Suppression of Vice set the figure at 80,000. Elsewhere, it has been estimated that there was one prostitute for every 12 males. By 1857, *The Lancet* reported a figure of 6,000 brothels in London. Virgins could earn a lucrative £25 for being 'deflowered' at a time when the annual wage for a skilled worker was £62.

FROM *HARRIS'S LIST OF COVENT GARDEN LADIES*, A PUBLICATION THAT ADVERTISED HIGH-CLASS PROSTITUTES:

'MISS B. NUMBER 18 OLD COMPTON STREET, SOHO.

This accomplished nymph has just attained her eighteenth year, and fraught with every perfection, enters a volunteer in the field of Venus. She plays on the pianoforte, sings, dances, and is the mistress of every manoeuver in the amorous contest that can enhance the coming pleasure; is of middle stature, fine auburn hair, dark eyes and very inviting countenance, which ever seems to beam delight and love. In bed she is all the heart can wish, or eyes admires every limb is symmetry, every action under cover truly amorous; her price two pounds.'

TORTURE CHAMBER

Mary Jeffries, a London madame, used to abduct children at stations while their parents were distracted. She catered to every vice. The *Pall Mall Gazette* reported, 'Flogging or birching goes on in brothels to a much greater degree than is generally believed. One of Mrs Jeffries' rooms was fitted up like a torture chamber; there were rings in the ceiling for hanging women and children up by the wrists, ladders for strapping them down at any angle, as well as the ordinary stretcher to which the victim is fastened so as to be unable to move. The instruments of flagellation included the ordinary birch, whips, holly branches and wire-thonged cat-o'-nine tails.'

Victorian London brothel terms

Abbess: the madame ❖ **Abbot:** the madame's husband ❖ **Judy:** prostitute ❖ **Dollymop:** part-time prostitute ❖ **Haymarket Hector:** pimp ❖ **Nebuchadnezzar:** male genitalia ❖ **Put Nebuchadnezzar out to grass:** sexual intercourse

VICTORIAN VALUES

▶ As late as 1900, many people still believed venereal disease could be cured by means of sexual intercourse with a virgin.

▶ William Blackstone set the tone for the Victorian era in the 18th century by defining a women's status: 'In law a husband and wife are one person, and the husband is that person.'

▶ In 1849, French surgeon Auguste Debay suggested that each organ had to be subjected to 'moderate exercise'. He also advised that sex should take place four times a week for a vigorous young man, instructing wives it was their duty 'to quell' their husbands' 'fires'.

▶ 'The rights and privileges of marriage' was a Victorian euphemism for 'brute sex' and sometimes rape.

▶ Until 1884, women could find themselves in jail for refusing to have sex with their husbands.

THE CRIMINAL LAW AMENDMENT ACT OF 1885

English journalist William Thomas Stead took on the issue of 'white slavery', or enforced prostitution. Following an undercover mission to bring the issue out into the open, his success cost him a period in jail. Arranging to buy Eliza Armstrong, the 13-year-old daughter of a chimney sweep, not only helped supply evidence for the Criminal Law Amendment Act of 1885, passed to protect women and minors, it also earned Stead three months in prison. MP Henry Labouchere then pushed the bill further to hit hard against prostitution in general and homosexuality in particular, leading to homophobic witch-hunts and the detention of thousands of men, including Oscar Wilde, who served two years with hard labour from 1895. Anal sex had been illegal since the reign of Henry VIII, but Labouchere ensured sexual conduct ill-befitting a gentleman was a slur on Christianity and punishable as gross indecency.

The Cleveland Street Scandal of 1889

Following an investigation into male prostitution and buggery, police discovered a telegraph delivery boy in possession of a suspicious amount of money, equal to several weeks' wages. 'I got the money from going to bed with a gentleman at his house,' the boy said of Charles Hammond, the owner of the targeted address. Hammond fled but his accomplice, Henry Newlove, revealed that two peers of the realm, Lord Arthur Somerset and Lord Euston, were regular clients of a male brothel in London. Later, it was alleged that Prince Eddy, the son of the Prince of Wales, was also involved.

'Sir Edward could contain himself no longer and, grasping Alice's head with both his hands, he pushed his weapon well into her mouth and spent down her throat.'

Extract from *The Yellow Room*, anonymous volume of Victorian erotica, 1891

Charles Dickens

As well as featuring fallen women in his novels *Oliver Twist* and *David Copperfield*, Charles Dickens was a campaigner for social justice. He wrote a leaflet to persuade prostitutes to come to Urania Cottage, a kind of rehabilitation centre he founded with friend Angela Burdett-Coutts in 1846.

FIVE VICTORIAN EROTIC CLASSICS

❖ LADY POKINGHAM *or* They All Do It – *diaries featured in the underground erotic magazine* The Pearl. *Sample text:* 'How I long to suck the sweets of love from your lips; to fondle and caress your lordly priapus, and feel its thrilling motions within me.'

❖ MY SECRET LIFE (THE SEX DIARY OF A VICTORIAN GENTLEMAN) *Memoir of 'Walter', who recorded sexual acts with 1,200 partners. No one knows who Walter was, though it's rumoured he was writer and book collector Henry Spencer Ashbee.*

❖ THE MYSTERIES OF VERBENA HOUSE: MISS BELLASIS BIRCHED FOR THIEVING *Only 150 copies of this luxury porn publication were printed.*

❖ THE WHIPPINGHAM PAPERS *by Algernon Charles Swinburne. Poetry and tales of flagellation by the respected poet, who signed with various pseudonyms, including* Etonensis.

❖ THE OYSTER EROTIC *With the demise of* The Pearl, *this underground magazine took over the role of celebrating characters such as Fanny Hill and Walter.*

It was perfectly acceptable and expected for a Victorian man to have sex with any woman as well as his wife, including prostitutes.

♦♦♦

A woman who had sexual contact with anyone other than her husband was labelled 'unclean' and a 'fallen woman'. She lost her reputation and her actions provided a valid excuse to be kicked out and divorced.

GAY LESBIAN BISEXUAL TRANSGENDER

Sex isn't always straightforward, but it is a natural urge, whatever your orientation, whatever turns you on. This applies across the spectrum, from physical attraction to feeling sexy in your own skin.

> The word 'homosexual' comes from the Greek 'homo' meaning 'same' and not the Latin 'homo' meaning 'man', and it is used to describe people who are attracted to members of the same sex.

YMCA

In 1978, the Village People celebrated the Young Men's Christian Association with their cheesy hit anthem 'YMCA' where 'you can have a good time… and hang out with all the boys'. From its arrival in the 19th century, 'the Y' provided one of the few places for gay men to meet sexual partners. It was actually set up in London in 1844 and in North America shortly after to take young single men's minds off immorality and, ironically, female temptation, promoting wholesome sex education instead. By the 20th century, rumours of unmasculine and licentious behaviour began to spread and upstanding members of the community, such as doctors and lawyers, were pinpointed in homosexual scandals. However, as one of the few places for gay men to meet, its popularity as a cruising outlet remained strong. In the 1960s, heterosexuality was championed via advertising campaigns and women were also allowed to become members, but by this time the gay community had begun to find its place in society and could go elsewhere. Nowadays, 'the Y' is still honoured for its part in gay history and the song continues to be enjoyed across the sexuality spectrum.

'Heterosexuality is not normal, it's just common.' Dorothy Parker

'Were kisses all the joys in bed,
one woman would another wed.'

From 'Sonnets to Sundry Notes of Music IV' by William Shakespeare

DECRIMINALIZATION

In 1967, coming out of the closet in the UK was made easier with the decriminalization of homosexual acts, which had been banned since 1885. However, this new freedom only applied within the privacy of the home and the age of consent was fixed at 21. Many gay acts were still viewed by the law under the label of 'gross indecency' and the number of arrests continued to rise. In 2000, the age of consent was set at 16 for both homosexuals and heterosexuals. In 2003, the act stated that buggery, cottaging, cruising and sex between more than two men were no longer crimes, while the term 'gross indecency' was removed in an effort to treat all types of sexual orientation equally.

Love island

The word 'lesbian', used to describe the love and attraction between women, comes from the poetry of Sappho who was born on the island of Lesbos in the seventh century BC. The first prominent female writer of ancient Greece, she is believed by many to have been bisexual as her love poems addressed both men and women. The island remains a popular destination for lesbian tourists.

'We were talking about the kissing in the movie. Clearly, it's pretty challenging material, but Ang said two men herding sheep was far more sexual than two men having sex on screen.'

Jake Gyllenhaal on *Brokeback Mountain* (2006)

Quickies

♦ Cave paintings and phallic objects suggesting acts of homoeroticism have been around since as far back as 12,000BC.

♦ In 1999, the Gaydar website phenomenon arrived, providing a global meeting place with profiles for gay and bisexual men and women.

♦ A 'tea engagement' is a liaison in a public toilet for the purpose of having sex.

♦ In the 1940s, studies by the Kinsey Institute suggested homosexual men had larger penises than heterosexual men.

♦ The 2005 Civil Partnerships Act meant that same-sex couples were entitled to the same legal rights as heterosexual couples.

♦ AC/DC is a term for bisexuality.

♦ Plato discusses homosexuality in his *Symposium* where he suggests love between men could in fact be superior to heterosexual love.

♦ In 2006, it was reported that archaeologists may have found the oldest painting of a gay kiss in an Egyptian tomb. The images showed the embrace normally used to show heterosexual love.

♦ Transgender is broadly defined as someone whose identity does not match the sex of their body. Sex-change operations can reassign the body, in whole or in part, to help that person live life as a member of their chosen sex.

♦ Lesbians have the lowest number of STD cases in sexually active adults.

♦ Transvestism or cross-dressing is the desire to wear clothes of the opposite sex, but this does not automatically define sexuality.

♦ Zephyrus and Hyakinthus were Greek lovers featured in the works of Homer and on pottery.

♦ Metrosexuals are straight men who appreciate lifestyle aesthetics usually associated with women and gay men, such as fashion, furniture and appearance.

COMING OUT TO THE MAINSTREAM

In 1981, Steven Carrington in *Dynasty* was the first US TV soap bisexual main character. In 1990, Zoe Tate from *Emmerdale* was the first lesbian character in a UK soap, while in 1992 Amanda Donohoe's bisexual character kissed a female colleague in *LA Law*, but the scene was shown from behind. In 1994, UK soap *Brookside* was the first to air a prime-time lesbian kiss between characters Beth and Margaret. Ellen DeGeneres received her highest ratings when she came out in 1997 in *Ellen*, her show about a woman who couldn't find the right man, which received a whole night of attention on Channel 4 in the UK. In 1996, Ross's ex, Carol, married girlfriend Susan in *Friends*. Award-winning TV sitcom *Will & Grace* brought homosexuality to the US mainstream from 1998. *Oranges Are Not the Only Fruit* by author Jeanette Winterson was a groundbreaking BBC drama, being the first to feature a lesbian

sex scene. Channel 4's 1999 drama *Queer As Folk* by Russell T Davies depicted a fantasy-cum-real gay life in Manchester, England, revealing promiscuous and sexually explicit content, including masturbation and 'rimming'. Its success inspired the US version and in 2002 the BBC's *Tipping the Velvet* dramatization was the first to do the same for lesbianism, followed by US drama *The L Word* in 2004: about lesbian and bisexual women, this broke the stereotypical butch-only image and introduced the term 'panty hamster', meaning vagina.

'A lot of what used to be known as gay culture –
broadly speaking, homoeroticism and being camp –
has been brought into mainstream culture.
I think we should be moving to an era where it's just sex.'
Neil Tennant, The Pet Shop Boys

MOUTH TO MOUTH

'I abhor the slimie kisse
(which to me most loathsome is).'
From *Kisses Loathsome* by Robert Herrick 1591–1674

The first erotic touch most people expect to experience, the kiss can be the most magical and most personal of all sexual contact, the archetypal fairy-tale ending or a taboo in prostitution.

K-I-S-S-I-N-G

Butterfly ○ do a fade-out ○ Eskimo ○ first base ○ Frenchy ○ kissletoe ○ lip action ○ lip salute ○ maw ○ pass secrets ○ peck ○ pucker up ○ smackeroonie ○ smooch ○ snog ○ suck face ○ swapping spit ○ throw the tongue ○ tongue sushi ○ tonsil hockey ○ tonsil swab ○ tulip sauce

---

'IT'S A PITY I CAN'T KISS MYSELF'

Sigmund Freud believed the origins of human sexual behaviour begin from birth. Sucking on a mother's breast or bottle is the first experience of satisfaction from nourishment, followed by a red-cheeked and full state, leading to the need for a rest. This appetite and its after-effects will be replaced by sexual needs and satisfaction in later life. Freud's theory also suggested that a baby's experience could explain a person's future kissing habits.

On the nose

When Thomas Saverland tried to kiss Caroline Newton in England in 1837, she bit part of his nose off, so he took her to court. The judge decreed any woman kissed against her will had the right to bite back.

'Kissing – and I mean like, yummy, smacking kissing – is the most delicious, most beautiful and passionate thing that two people can do, bar none. Better than sex, hands down.' Drew Barrymore

Kissing record

In June 2007, 12,800 pairs of lips made contact outside Parliament in Budapest, Hungary, which secured victory over the Philippines, who had taken the record for simultaneous kissing a few months before.

LIP SERVICE

*Kissing was first recorded in Vedic Sanskrit texts in India around 1500*BC *✻ Kisses under the mistletoe in the Middle Ages implied commitment and sometimes that a couple were engaged ✻ The French were the first to introduce kissing as part of courtship in the 6th century ✻ It is illegal for a husband to kiss his wife on a Sunday in Connecticut ✻ James Belshaw and Sophia Severin kissed non-stop for 31 hours, 30 minutes and 30 seconds in Oxford Street, London, ending on 7 July 2005 ✻ Alfred Wolfram of Minnesota, USA, holds the Guinness record for the most kisses: 8,001 people in eight hours ✻ Legend has it that any woman who kisses the statue of 16th century soldier Guidarello Guidarelli in Ravenna, Italy will marry a wonderful man. His lips have become blushed from the touch of more than five million hopefuls.*

LoveFilm named the moment between Heath Ledger and Jake Gyllenhaal in *Brokeback Mountain* as the best screen kiss ever.

♦♦♦

Giambattista Basile's original story of Sleeping Beauty, called *Sun, Moon and Talia* from 1634, has no happy-ever-after awakening kiss. The handsome prince is a king who rapes her instead.

GAGGING FOR IT

Sex is possibly the easiest target and the biggest
butt of all jokes… suddenly, everyone's a comedian.

'Sex is identical to comedy in
that it involves timing.'
Phyllis Diller

'If sex isn't a joke, what is?'
Nella Larsen

'A really hard laugh is like sex –
one of the ultimate diversions
of existence.' Jerry Seinfeld

'Think of me as Chomsky with
dick jokes.' Bill Hicks

'Bisexuality doubles your
chances of a date on Saturday
night.' Rodney Dangerfield

'I married a German. Every
night I dress up as Poland and
he invades me.' Bette Midler

'It's hard to be funny when you
have to be clean.' Mae West

'When authorities warn you of
the sinfulness of sex, there is an
important lesson to be learned.
Do not have sex with the
authorities.' Matt Groening

'I want to tell you a terrific
story about oral contraception.
I asked this girl to sleep with
me and she said no.'
Woody Allen

'Before we make love, my
husband takes a pain killer.'
Joan Rivers

> *'I'm a girl who lost her reputation and never missed it.'* Mae West

MAE WEST (1893–1980) was a past mistress of innuendo and the eight-inch platform walk. She challenged the rules, was bold, raunchy and vulgar, and successfully delivered the message that women enjoy sexual attention too. She also left a trail of unique one-liners, from the classic 'Come up and see me some time' to the one and only 'Is that a gun in your pocket or are you just happy to see me?' Her 1926 play *Sex*, which she wrote and starred in, about a hooker looking to get away from it all with a rich husband, landed her in court for obscenity. West was sent to the can for 10 days, where she was allowed to wear silk instead of prison underwear. *Sex* reopened off-Broadway in 1999.

> *'Whoever named it necking was a poor judge of anatomy.'*
> Groucho Marx

THE ARISTOCRATS (2005)

A film about a cult sex joke, it features 100 of the biggest names in the funny business, each giving their personal rendition and adding a twist on an old and filthy burlesque joke

shared only by a magic circle of comedians but never told in public. Too rude and lewd for the stage, the idea is to keep outdoing the previous account, resulting in more and more extreme versions. Joke-tellers include Whoopi Goldberg, Eric Idle, Eddie Izzard, Harry Shearer, Carrie Fisher, Robin Williams and Billy Connolly.

STRANGE FASCINATION

'The only unnatural sex act is that which you cannot perform.'
Alfred Kinsey, 1966

APPARENTLY...

▶ When his partner reached orgasm, he liked her to throw a pie in his face.

▶ A wet suit, gas mask and hot water bottles hanging from string around the neck was the favoured outfit of a

man caught exposing himself.

▶ Fortunately, before their wedding, a man discovered his bride-to-be was actually his daughter via artificial insemination from his own donated sperm.

MORE KICKS THAN PRICKS

AXILLISM Sexual activity using a partner's armpit as a substitute 'vessel' for the vagina.

ANACLITISM Sexual arousal from contact with objects associated with infancy, which can involve the wearing of nappies/diapers. Also known as infantilism, practitioners act out 'adult baby' fantasies.

OMORASHI Mainly Japanese phenomenon, where a full bladder and wetting oneself in public causes arousal. Game shows and sex trade workers in Japan cater in large numbers to this fetish. Followers can also turn to *Wet Set Magazine*, an Australian-based publication aimed mainly at western practitioners.

TAMAKERI Another Japanese contribution to sexual culture: the desire to watch a woman kick a man in the testicles, which has a healthy porn industry to cater to it.

LEGAL TECHNICALITIES... ALLEGEDLY

✵ Making love while hunting or fishing on your wedding day is against the law in Oblong, Illinois.

✵ Women are not permitted to wear patent leather shoes in Cleveland, Ohio, in case they reflect regions of the body that should be private from strangers.

✵ It's illegal to ask a gas attendant to 'fill her up' after dark in Geneva, New York.

✵ A woman cannot strip off in front of a picture of a man in Oxford, Ohio.

✵ Men are not allowed to be sexually aroused in public in Mississippi. Promoting the use of or owning more than six dildos can lay you open to a felony charge.

✵ Moose are not allowed to have sex on the streets of Fairbanks, Alaska.

✵ And pigs might fly but... they are not permitted to have sex on airport property in Kingsville, Texas.

Car Lover

Sex in the back of a car is not unusual, however. A recent report in British newspaper *The Sun* told of a British mechanic who enjoys sex with the car itself. A fan of *Knightrider* as a boy, the signs of this unusual fetish began when Chris Donald noticed human characteristics in cars and experienced emotional feelings towards them. As well as real relationships, he has formed attachments to a number of vehicles – including a Peugeot called Laura – having sex with more than 30 in 20 years. Experts call out-of-the-ordinary types of desire 'paraphilia', but this is not something that needs treatment. Chris has met several other motor enthusiasts, shared moments of engine arousal and has written a book called *How to Make Love to a Car*.

'RHYTHM METHOD'

'There's people making babies to my music. That's nice.' Barry White

The food of love has played on since man first found his beat. A million love songs later, from Brahms' red light performances to Elvis's gyrating hips and beyond, the world continues to get it on to music.

The facts of 'rock and roll'

Origin: black slang for dancing and sex: rock = shake up, roll = having sex
Rocking: used to mean 'rapture' by black gospel singers
Roll in the Hay: sexual phrase used in literature for hundreds of years
First Time on Record: in 1916, 'rocking and rolling' featured as a spiritual term in Male Quartette 'The Camp Meeting Jubilee'; in 1922 Trixie Smith's 'My Baby Rocks Me With One Steady Roll' was the first to use the terms for their sexual meaning
Double Entendre: used in the 1940s as dancing with underlying ideas of sex in 'race music' songs such as 'Good Rocking Tonight' by Roy Brown.

ROLLING STONE'S ROCK & ROLL DAILY TOP FIVE SEXIEST SONGS EVER

'Let's Get It On' *Marvin Gaye, 1973* ❖ 'Closer' *Nine Inch Nails, 1993* ❖ 'Darling Nikki' *Prince, 1984* ❖ 'Like A Virgin' *Madonna, 1984* ❖ 'Get Up (I Feel Like Being a) Sex Machine' *James Brown, 1970*

TOP 10 SEXIEST SONGS… NOT ACTUALLY ABOUT SEX

'Got to Give it Up, Pt1' *Marvin Gaye, 1977* ❖ 'Love Theme from Spartacus' *Bill Evans, 1960* ❖ 'Body II Body' *Samantha Mumba, 2000* ❖ 'Kickstart My Heart' *Motley Crue, 1989* ❖ 'A Girl Like You' *Edwyn Collins, 1994* ❖ 'Party Hard' *Pulp, 1998* ❖ 'See No Evil' *Television, 1977* ❖ 'Lit Up' *Buckcherry, 1999* ❖ 'Lean Lanky Daddy' *Little Ann* ❖ 'The Immigrant Song' *Led Zeppelin, 1970* Source: *Stylus* magazine's Staff Top 10

BANNED

●**1940s** Due to its suggestive lyrics, George Formby's 'When I'm Cleaning Windows' is initially banned by BBC radio: 'The blushing bride she looks divine/ The bridegroom he is doing fine/ I'd rather have his job than mine/ When I'm Cleaning Windows'

●**1951** 'Wham! Bam! Thank You, Ma'am' by Dean Martin is deemed suggestive and therefore banned from US radio

●**1954** Rosemary Clooney's 'Mambo Italiano' is considered in poor taste by ABC

●**1955** Elvis is threatened with arrest if he moves during his performances in San Diego and Florida

●**1956** Cameramen are instructed to only show Elvis from the waist up on *The Ed Sullivan Show*

●**1962** Catholic kids are forbidden to dance to 'The Twist' as New York's Bishop Burke says it is lewd

●**1965** PJ Proby's invitation to perform on *Shingdig* is revoked following his pants splitting at a European gig

●**1967** Van Morrison's original version of 'Brown-Eyed Girl' doesn't get airplay due to its content of premarital sex and teenage pregnancy

●**1976** RKO insists the line 'spread your wings and let me come inside' is cut before they will play Rod Stewart's 'Tonight's the Night'

●**1977** The Sex Pistols are denied visas for their first American tour

●**1981** Stations in Provo and Salt Lake City feel their Mormon audience will find 'Physical' by Olivia Newton-John too risqué

●**1987** George Michael's 'I Want Your Sex' is banned by a number of US radio stations

Band Names with Sexual Content

The Enormous Horns ❖ Sex Pistols ❖ Celibate Rifles ❖ The Slits ❖ Queen ❖ Tool ❖ Helmet ❖ Fanny ❖ Fudge Tunnel ❖ Revolting Cocks ❖ Machine Gun Fellatio ❖ Butthole Surfers ❖ Kiss ❖ Orgy ❖ The Four Skins

'The way it felt between your thighs/ Pleasure that made you cry.'
Maroon 5, 'Makes Me Wonder', 2007

Too much too young?

In 2006, a report in the *Journal of the American Academy of Pediatrics* suggested music could encourage teens to have sex early. A telephone survey from 2002 to 2005 by the Rand Corporation think tank found that kids who listened to sexually degrading lyrics were twice as likely to have sex within the next two years as those who were innocent about songs where females are sex objects and males are studs. It revealed boys were being taught to be ruthless in the chase, while girls were learning it was OK to be submissive and disrespected. Some kids said they just liked the beat.

WHAT'S IN A NAME?

10cc *quantity of semen ejaculated by the average male is 9cc* ♦ **24-7 Spyz** *always looking for sex* ♦ **311** *police code for indecent exposure* ♦ **Breeders** *gay slang for heterosexuals* ♦ **Buzzcocks** *vibrators* ♦ **Captain Beefheart** *Don Van Vliet's uncle exposed himself, then squeezed till his penis turned purple 'like a big ole beefheart'* ♦ **Cinderella** *named after a porn movie* ♦ **Huffamoose** *Canadian slang for blowjob* ♦ **Irving Claw Trio** *Bettie Page 'Pin-up King' photographer* ♦ **Jelly Roll Morton** *'Jelly Roll' is slang for penis* ♦ **LL Cool J** *Ladies Love Cool James* ♦ **Pearl Jam** *As kids, the boys gave the name to Eddie's grandma's peyote jam. Also slang for sperm* ♦ **The Pogues** *short for original name Pogue Mahone, from* Póg Mo Thóin, *the Irish Gaelic for 'kiss my arse'* ♦ **Professor Longhair** *whorehouse pianists were called professors* ♦ **Skyclad** *pagan word meaning naked* ♦ **Steely Dan** *literary reference from William Burrough's* Naked Lunch *to a metal dildo crushed by an evil prostitute's genitals* ♦ **Throbbing Gristle** *Yorkshire slang for erection* ♦ **To Live and Shave in LA** *Ron Jeremy porn movie* ♦ **Velvet Underground** *Title of an S&M book found on a New York sidewalk* ♦ **WASP** *We are sex perverts*

CURIOUS FACTS

❖ Eric Burdon of The Animals used to crack eggs on to the bodies of women he made love to. He was nicknamed the Egg Man – which Lennon later used in the lyric of 'I Am The Walrus' (1967)

❖ Pink Floyd's 'Arnold Layne' (1976) is about a man stealing women's clothes and was banned by Radio London for being too dirty

❖ Eric Clapton fell in love with his best friend's wife – the friend being George Harrison, the wife Patti. He asked George if he could have her and George said yes. Eric and Patti married in 1979. Harrison wrote 'Something' (1969) about her; Clapton wrote 'Layla' (1970) about her

❖ John Lennon and Yoko Ono held a weeklong honeymoon 'bed-in' for peace in Room 702 at the Amsterdam Hilton in 1969 and in 1970 they started a sex-change hoax

❖ The Parental Advisory label has been used in America since 1985 and Britain since 1995

❖ Bow Wow Wow singer Annabella posed nearly nude on the cover of *Your Cassette Pet* (1980) at the age of 14, getting svengali Malcolm McLaren into plenty of trouble with her mother. The following year she appeared nude on their second album *See Jungle! See Jungle! Go Join Your Gang Yeah! City All Over, Go Ape Crazy!* (1981)

Music Lovers

Sonny and Cher ❖ ABBA ❖ Carly Simon and James Taylor ❖ Stevie Wonder and Syreeta ❖ Ashford and Simpson ❖ Paul and Linda McCartney ❖ Smokey and Claudette Robinson ❖ Debbie Harry and Chris Stein ❖ Britney Spears and Justin Timberlake ❖ Jessica Simpson and Nick Lachey

'Music, not sex, got me aroused.' Marvin Gaye

'They want my treasure so they get their pleasures from my photo.'

Fergie, 'Fergalicious', 2006

✳

'She's hopped up on me/ I've got her in my zone/ Her body's pressed up on me/ I think she's ready to blow.'

Justin Timberlake, 'Future Sex Love Sound', 2006

GENDER BLENDER

'You got your mother in a whirl/ She's not sure if you're a boy or a girl.' David Bowie, 'Rebel Rebel', 1974

♦ *In the 70s, David Bowie's sexuality was expressed through the stages of his music, including early Mod lipstick and sharp suit look, and the redhead glam-punk Ziggy Stardust*

♦ *He was a massive fan of Little Richard and Syd Barrett who both wore make-up*

♦ *Met wife Angie when reportedly they were both having sex with the same man. She was bisexual and it is said they spent the night before their wedding in 1970 in bed with a friend*

♦ *In 1971, Bowie caused a stir by dressing as a woman for the cover of* The Man Who Sold the World. *He said he was wearing his 'man dress'*

♦ *His sexual experiences and experimentation caused an 'is he or isn't he?' furore, with reports of*

sexual liaisons with men and women

♦ *In April 1971, he told the* Daily Mail *he wasn't gay. In 1972, he told* Melody Maker *he was. In 1976,* Playboy *revealed he was bisexual*

♦ *In 1978, he starred in the film* Just a Gigolo *where he played a male escort providing sexual services in a Berlin brothel; he said he did it to meet Marlene Dietrich who played the Madame, but he never did*

♦ *In 1993, he called himself a 'closet heterosexual'*

♦ *In 1992, he married model Iman*

♦ *In 2002, he told* Blender *he had no problem being bisexual, just didn't want to 'hold any banners or be a representative of any group of people'; he wanted to be a songwriter and performer*

Frankie Goes to Hollywood: 'Relax' 1983

The number one banned by the BBC because of its 'sexually explicit lyrics': 'Relax, don't do it, when you want to sock it to it/Relax, don't do it, when you want to come'. Called 'overtly obscene' by Radio 1 DJ Mike Read, the gushing noises at the end were believed to represent sexual climax. The 12in 'Sex Mix' received complaints due to its apparently sexual sound effects. The original video was filmed in an S&M theme gay club; it was banned by the BBC and MTV. All this time, the band said the song was actually about motivation.

SEXY COVERS

The following albums are recognized for baring all, or almost:
Roxy Music *Roxy Music* (1972) ⌘ Prince *Lovesexy* (1989) ⌘ Basement Jaxx *Remedy* (1999) ⌘ Nancy Sinatra *Sugar* (1966) ⌘ Ice T *Gangsta Rap* (2006) ⌘ Sugar Ray *Lemonade & Brownies* (1995) ⌘ Herb Alpert & the Tijuana Brass *Whipped Cream & Other Delights* (1965) ⌘ Rollins Band *Nice* (2001) ⌘ John Lennon and Yoko Ono posed naked on the *Two Virgins* album cover (1968) and were seen from behind on the back – 30,000 copies were seized by police in New York ⌘ *Blind Faith* (1969) by Blind Faith caused a scandal as it had an underage girl exposing her chest ⌘ *Diamond Dogs* originally had the Bowiedog's genitals showing on the back cover, until it was airbrushed out ⌘ The *Woodstock* (soundtrack) album (1970) depicts a couple under covers on the front and a naked couple on the back ⌘ The original cover for *Electric Ladyland* (1968) by Jimi Hendrix depicted naked women, but this was banned in the US.

PLAYBOY

Mariah Carey, Dannii Minogue, Britney Spears, Dolly Parton and Jennifer Lopez have all appeared on the cover ⌘ Lil Jon, Nelly and Flavor Flav have all been guest photographers ⌘ Tiffany and Debbie Gibson posed to show they weren't teens anymore – in the 2000s ⌘ Weezer filmed their 'Beverley Hills' video at the Playboy Mansion.

MADONNA SEX TIMELINE

'I'll give you love
I'll hit you like a truck
I'll give you love
I'll teach you how to... aahh'
Madonna, 'Erotica', 1992

✠ **1970s** Introduced to gay discos by ballet teacher, friends with drag queens and rent boys

✠ **1978** Appears topless and in a rape scene in low-budget movie *A Certain Sacrifice*. Works as a nude model

✠ **1980s** One of first celebrities to support AIDS causes

1983 Shows her midriff in 'Lucky Star', which causes concern as fans copy the fashion

✠ **1985** Performs 'Like A Virgin' at the MTV Music Video Awards on top of a wedding cake, wearing a white wedding dress and 'Boy Toy' belt, as she writhes around exposing sexy lingerie and simulating sexual pleasure

✠ **1985** Black and white nude pictures in *Playboy* and *Penthouse* bought from a photographer she had once posed for

✠ **1987** The Pope calls for boycott of *Who's That Girl* World Tour due to sexual content and costume, including revealing 'kiss' on her knickers and flirting with a teenage boy. Debate over portrayal of underage corruption as a minor tries to get into a strip club and kisses her in 'Open Your Heart' video

✠ **1988** Speculation about sexual assault by husband Sean Penn

✠ **1989** Penn and new partner pregnant; she is reported to have sent a note saying, 'Silly boy, if you'd given me a baby, we'd still be together'. 'Like A Prayer' video mixes sex and religion offending Pope and Pepsi

✠ **1990** 'Vogue' inspired by underground dance in gay clubs called 'voguing'. 'Hanky Panky' causes controversy as it implies she enjoys spanking. Blonde Ambition World Tour contains sex and Catholicism themes, as well as simulated masturbation after she is touched up by male dancers. This triggers another call from the Pope for a boycott. Toronto police threaten action if lewd content isn't changed. It isn't and there are no charges. Jean-Paul Gaultier's cone bra becomes an iconic design. Live on BBC Radio 1, she holds the record for profanities uttered before the watershed, with 24 'fucks', so she's banned from live performances on the BBC. Provocative video for 'Justify My Love' features homosexuality and S&M at a Paris hotel and is one of first to be banned by MTV

✤ **1991** *In Bed with Madonna* (originally *Truth or Dare*) film, with the truth-or-dare oral sex with a bottle, showing her breasts and admitting Sean Penn is the love of her life

✤ **1992** *Erotica* is her first album to get Parental Advisory label. Video is MTV's second to be banned. 'Deeper and Deeper' is about a young man coming out. *Sex* goes on sale containing adult softcore images, fetishism, lesbianism, homosexuality, S&M, anilingus and rape; it's the most successful coffee table title ever published

✤ **1993** The Girlie Show World Tour is inspired by artist Edward Hopper's burlesque painting. Madonna dresses as a dominatrix, spanks dancers' bottoms and is surrounded by topless performers and depictions of orgies. Rubs the Puerto Rican flag between her legs. Politician in Germany and Orthodox Jews in Israel call for a boycott of shows due to pornographic imagery. Stars in erotic thriller *Body of Evidence*

✤ **1994** Says 'fuck' 13 times on *The Late Show with David Letterman*

✤ **1997** 'You Must Love Me' from *Evita* wins Best Original Song Oscar

✤ **2002** MTV2 names 'Justify My Love' as number two most controversial video ever behind The Prodigy's number one, 'Smack My Bitch Up'

✤ **2003** Kisses Britney Spears and Christina Aguilera at the MTV Video Music Awards

✤ **2005** BBC airs Live 8 concert where she begins with 'Are you fucking ready London?'

✤ **2006** Removes middle finger gesture from 'Sorry' video to get airplay

✤ **2006** *Confessions* Tour, two dancers, one bearing a Jewish symbol and the other a Muslim symbol painted on their chests kiss as she asks for world peace – this is controversial as homosexuality is a powerful taboo in most of the Middle East

THE 1960S REVOLUTION

'Basically, the thing at the time, you used to just try and find girls that would fuck. The rest of it was just, you know. I mean, it wasn't quite as easy then as it is now. Since the invention of the Pill, it's become much easier.' Mick Jagger

The contraceptive pill was first released in Puerto Rico in 1956, then the US in 1960. It was not approved for use in Japan until 1999. Today, more than 100 million women worldwide take the Pill.

Porn mags

👁 At the beginning of the 1960s, men read *National Geographic* as a source of titillation – namely the anthropological articles from Africa illustrated with bare-breasted women.

👁 Ditto *Health and Efficiency*. That is how desperate things were.

👁 *Lady Chatterley's Lover* by DH Lawrence was given the green light in 1960 in the UK, when the obscenity case against it was declared unfounded. This paved the way for a change in the laws and the public perception of what constituted pornography.

👁 *Fiesta* – founded in 1966 in Britain. Dubbed 'the magazine for men that women love to read', *Fiesta*'s most famous contribution is its Readers' Wives page.

👁 *Penthouse* – founded in 1965, it occupies the middle ground between *Playboy* and *Hustler*.

👁 *Mayfair* – founded in 1965 in Britain in response to *Playboy* and *Penthouse*, remained relatively tame until the 1990s.

👁 *Private* – founded in 1965 in Sweden as the world's first full-colour, hardcore pornographic magazine.

'You don't think I enjoyed what we did this evening, do you? What I did tonight was for Queen and country!' James Bond, *Thunderball*, 1965

BUNNY GIRL RULES

Bunny girls were waitresses employed at Playboy clubs which were open between 1960 and 1988. Training included posture, how to carry a tray, how to order drinks and the Bunny Dip – how to bend over tables without breasts falling out of the costume. Bunny Mother carried out inspections before shifts, ensuring high standards of fluffy tails, perfect nails and all-round presentation of costume – corset, cuffs, ears. It was hard work and pay was about £1 an hour. Under no circumstances were 'guests' allowed to touch Bunnies' tails. The penalty for this was instant expulsion.

Make love not war

The origins of this saying go back to 1960s America, and protestors against the Vietnam War, rebellious students and hippies – all supporters of the sexual revolution. There is no record of its actual creator, but it is associated with the writings of Herbert Marcuse, a guru from the Frankfurt school of thought.

ICONS OF THE ERA

ROGER VADIM AND BRIGITTE BARDOT *golden couple of 1960s French cinema, collaborating on* Et Dieu Créa La Femme. ♥ ROGER VADIM AND JANE FONDA *the director and his third wife made* Barbarella, *a sci-fi sex romp, in 1968.* ♥ SERGE GAINSBOURGH AND JANE BIRKIN *immortalized by their song* 'Je T'Aime… Moi Non Plus', *1969, which contained the sounds of a female orgasm.* ♥ RICHARD BURTON AND LIZ TAYLOR *Hollywood's golden couple, who married and divorced each other twice, starred as the ancient lovers Mark Antony and Cleopatra in the 1963 film.* ♥ SEAN CONNERY AND IAN FLEMING *no, not a couple, but the former Edinburgh milkman gave the novelist's creation, the jet-setting spy James Bond, a larger-than-life sex appeal on the big screen.*

THE ONE-EYED TROUSER SNAKE

The penis – ultimate male symbol, provider of pleasure, victim of ridicule, worshipped throughout history, envied and reviled – it's a lot to take in.

TEN FACTS ABOUT THE PENIS

1 *Ancient Romans wore phallic talismans to ward off the evil eye.*

2 *'Boners' have no bones.*

3 *Men under 50 have erections every 70 to 100 minutes during sleep.*

4 *The average speed of ejaculation is about 28 miles an hour.*

5 *In 1609, a Dr Wecker discovered a body with two penises in Bologna and about 80 more cases have since been reported.*

6 *The average number of daily erections is 11, with 9 in the night.*

7 *Erotic feelings travel at 156 miles an hour from the skin to the brain.*

8 *When greeting each other, the Walibri tribe of central Australia shake penises.*

9 *The 20 cm-long Ice Age Hohle Fels phallus is the oldest representation of a penis at 28,000 years old.*

10 *Alfred Kinsey reported a penis that was 2.5 cm (1 inch) long when fully erect which makes it one of the smallest (normally developed) penises on record.*

Nicknames

All-beef sausage ✳ bald-headed hermit ✳ Big Ben ✳ belt-buster ✳ best of three ✳ blue-veined custard chucker ✳ Captain Hightop the Love Commander ✳ dangling participle ✳ donniker ✳ drumstick ✳ eager pleaser ✳ eleventh finger ✳ finger puppet ✳ girlometer ✳ hairless wonder ✳ lady's delight ✳ Little Elvis ✳ love dart ✳ lust bone ✳ marriage gear ✳ natural member ✳ nutty buddy ✳ one-eyed trouser snake ✳ peacemaker ✳ peppermint stick ✳ purple lollipop ✳ red lobster ✳ schmeegle ✳ spitting cobra ✳ stemmer ✳ stocking stuffer ✳ tonsil wrench ✳ underpant eel ✳ wazzock ✳ whanger ✳ woofer ✳ virgin's dream

DOES SIZE MATTER?

British urologists Kevan Wylie and Ian Eardley's review of more than 50 studies since the 1940s into 'small penis syndrome' (SPS), published in June 2007, found that men have more sexual confidence if they have a large penis. Their findings? Women are more interested in looks and character, and width rather than length. While 85 per cent of women are happy with their partner's size, only 55 per cent of men are satisfied. The average erect penis is about 5.5 inches to 6.2 inches long and 4.7 to 5.1 inches in girth. Penis size does not differ according to race or reduce in size in older men. In the 1940s, the Kinsey Institute found homosexual men had larger penises than heterosexual men. The condition of SPS is more common in men of average size than those with small penises, and is blamed on comparisons made with erotic imagery during youth.

'Sometimes the only thing we women want is a dick and no arguments. What could make us happier?' Linda Fiorentino, actress

Penis-Lengthening Methods
Penis pump suction ✳ Jelqing increases blood pressure and is also called 'milking' ✳ Indian holy men and Sadhus attach weights ✳ Dayak men in Borneo puncture the testicles and attach stimulators ✳ Brazil's Topinama tribe got poisonous snakes to bite their penises which hurt like hell but made them larger ✳ Extenders ✳ Stretching ✳ Hanging weights, a method thought to have been used by African tribes up to 2,000 years ago ✳ Clamping ✳ Silicone injection ✳ the Mambas of the New Hebrides wrap them in yards of cloth ✳ Implants ✳ Therapy ✳ Trimming pubic hair and weight loss give the impression of enlargement ✳ Genital beading in Indonesia and south Asia, includes implants of ball bearings, studs and rings ✳ An Amazonian wedding ritual involves covering the penis with bamboo filled with bees.

SPAM

❀ Billions of emails offering pills and other devices used by supposed 'millions of happy customers around the world' claim to enlarge the penis and cure impotence so users can 'get the perfect feeling of being a man again' ❀ Double Standards Penis Patch made number two in AOL's 2005 Top 10 global spam subject lines ❀ In 2003, penis enlargement was the number one spam email according to Brightmail, while Viagra was number two ❀ Developed by Dr Long Daochao in the 1980s, penis enlargement surgery can be legally performed by one of only 30 registered doctors in the US.

15 March is penis party time in Japan. Hounen Matsuri is celebrated with a giant wooden phallus parade, dildos and penis-shaped chocolates.

♦♦♦

Eating broccoli makes semen taste bitter.

'Hooray for your one-eyed trouser snake
Your piece of pork, your wife's best friend,
your Percy or your cock
You can wrap it up in ribbons, you can stuff it in your sock
But don't take it out in public or they'll stick you in the dock and
you won't come back.'

'The Penis Song' by Eric Idle from *Monty Python's The Meaning of Life* (1983)

According to the Kinsey report, the youngest age at which the normal male first ejaculates is eight and the oldest, for the same event, is 21.

THANKS FOR THE MAMMARIES

Breasts – symbols of fertility and femininity, survival and pleasure, prominent in many fields from politics to porn, big ones, small ones, an obsession to many in Western culture, sexually irrelevant to others – there's more to them than meets the eye.

'I'm a normal, red-blooded American man. I like to look at naked women. I love breasts, any kind. I love 'em! Boobs, bazooms, balloons, bags, bazongas. The bigger, the better. Nipples like udders, nipples like saucers, big pale rosy-brown nipples. Little bitty baby nipples. Real or fake, what's the difference? I like tits. Who's kidding who? Tits are great!' Greg Kinnear in *Auto Focus* (2002)

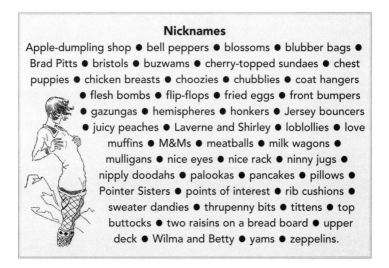

Nicknames

Apple-dumpling shop • bell peppers • blossoms • blubber bags • Brad Pitts • bristols • buzwams • cherry-topped sundaes • chest puppies • chicken breasts • choozies • chubblies • coat hangers • flesh bombs • flip-flops • fried eggs • front bumpers • gazungas • hemispheres • honkers • Jersey bouncers • juicy peaches • Laverne and Shirley • loblollies • love muffins • M&Ms • meatballs • milk wagons • mulligans • nice eyes • nice rack • ninny jugs • nipply doodahs • palookas • pancakes • pillows • Pointer Sisters • points of interest • rib cushions • sweater dandies • thrupenny bits • tittens • top buttocks • two raisins on a bread board • upper deck • Wilma and Betty • yams • zeppelins.

'People think you can't be clever if you have breasts.'
TV presenter Kelly Brook

COVER STORY

Western cultures hide the breast, mainly the nipple, while in some African and South Pacific cultures the bare breast has been a non-sexualized everyday sight. Commentators have suggested that the western taboo that has led to the covering up of the breast has stimulated man's appetite for wanting what he doesn't have. Going back to 2,500BC in Crete, Minoan women wore clothing to hold up their breasts. However, in ancient Rome and Greece, they let them hang loose under shapeless garments, while the Church of the Middle Ages barely recognized the female form. The contrived fashion for cleavage is a relatively modern idea. It was only around the 15th century that the undergarment was even introduced and artists began to eroticize the breasts, while women were encouraged to use them to bond with their children and their husbands. Renaissance corsets went from flattening the breasts to pushing them up in the long-standing style of décolletage. The invention of the bra by Herminie Cadolle came at the turn of the 20th century, but the breast bucket, over-the-shoulder boulder-holder, booby trap, double-barrelled slingshot, tit hammock, upper-decker-flopper-stopper, call it what you will, was patented in 1913 by New Yorker Mary Phelps-Jacobs, who used two handkerchiefs and a pink ribbon to avoid the discomfort of the corset. In 1914, she sold the rights to the Warner Brothers Corset Company for $1,500. The 1920s saw the rise of the flat chest and boyish figures, while in the 1940s and 1950s breasts were promoted by 'sweater girls' such as Lana Turner and Jane Russell, whose assets inspired a Howard Hughes aerodynamic underwire bra. Jayne Mansfield, the 'working man's Monroe', said people were more interested in her 40.21.35 than her IQ. In the 1960s, breasts were shown off when a bra-less fashion movement was led by Yves Saint-Laurent's sheer blouse and feminists who 'burned' their bras. Madonna's cone bra by Jean-Paul Gaultier and the return of cleavage marked the 1990s and, in the 21st century, new styles, plus silicone gel and the 'chicken fillet', arrived to fill up and push out, and augmentation through surgery began.

IMPLANT ICONS

❋ Katie Price, aka Jordan, the queen of British glamour modelling, made a career from her breasts, first appearing as a Page 3 pin-up in *The Sun* newspaper, a platform for the nation's breasts, and then in men's magazines, including *Playboy*. She had surgery to increase her breast size to (according to husband Peter Andre) 'just 32FF', although Page 3 now has a natural-only policy. In 2001's British General Election, she ran as a candidate promising free implants and nudist beaches.

❋ Pamela Anderson's breasts first received mass adulation on-screen and then on the pitch at a Canadian football game. She became a *Playboy* playmate, then starred in *Baywatch*, her breasts becoming synonymous with red swimsuits the world over. In 2005, she pole-danced topless, with painted stars, in Elton John's *'The Red Piano'* video.

Breast of the rest

Amazonian women were thought to have cut off a breast to make it easier to draw a bow. ✧ Bubby-smoochers and mastophallators are men who enjoy sexual release between the breasts. ✧ Tit torture includes a breast press made of adjustable bars forced down on to the chest of female masochists to chain wrap or clamp the nipples. ✧ The practice of breast binding goes back to about 2,500BC. ✧ Breast form is an advanced prosthetic resembling the feel, weight and movement of a natural breast.

'At school my boobs were bigger than all my friends' and I was afraid to show them. Now, I feel they make my outfits look better. They're like an accessory.' Jessica Simpson

THE SEX INDUSTRY

'Thou rascal beadle, hold thy bloody hand!
Why dost thou lash that whore? Strip thine own back;
Thou hotly lust'st to use her in that kind
For which thou whipp'st her.'
Shakespeare, *King Lear*, 1605

It's a job and someone has always done it. Yet prostitution remains one of the most stigmatized professions, despite its continuing ability to drum up custom.

FACTS AND FIGURES

Estimated worldwide revenue for the sex and porn industry (2006): $97 billion; US (2006): $13.3 billion ♦ *'sex' is the number one term used on search engine sites; 'pornography/porn' is fourth* ♦ *Hollywood releases 11,000 adult movies annually, more than 20 times its mainstream production* ♦ *72 million 'unique visitors' clicked on adult websites per month worldwide in 2006; 40 million of these were Americans; 77 per cent of visitors to adult websites are male* ♦ *55 per cent of films rented in US hotels in 2005 were porn movies; 12 minutes was the average viewing time* ♦ *The porn industry in California employs over 12,000 workers, yielding some $36 million annually in taxes* ♦ *Over 30 per cent of 1,500 companies surveyed have sacked employees for 'inappropriate use' of the internet* ♦ *In a 2000* Christianity Today *survey, 33 per cent of clergy admitted visiting a sexually explicit website.*

Sex Directory

Between 1757 and 1795, failed Irish poet and bankrupt Sam Derrick anonymously published *Harris's List of Covent Garden Ladies*, an almanac of the area's prostitutes (see p.50). It included addresses and prices, as well as witty descriptions of the ladies and their services.

'I believe that sex is one of the most beautiful, natural, wholesome things that money can buy.' Steve Martin

A survey of 3,000 men in Britain by *Club International* in 2006 revealed that 7 per cent – the equivalent of 1.5 million men nationwide – visit prostitutes four times a year and pay about £61 a time. A third are constantly worried their secret will be discovered, while 90 per cent love their partners and, of these, 80 per cent say their sex life is dull and the reason they use hookers in the first place.

THE OLDEST PROFESSION?

Prostitution may have originated as a respectable and spiritual transaction between priestesses and priests in Babylonian temples. It was designed to bring them closer to God, with no money changing hands. The first brothels were probably in Egypt, but they evidently became popular in ancient Greece, where prostitutes, mostly women and teenage boys, were obliged to wear distinctive clothing and pay taxes. They advertised their services on their sandals, which left the words 'follow me' imprinted in the sand. In Rome, the ranks of the sex trade were made up mainly of foreign slaves, abandoned children and criminal women. In Europe in the Middle Ages, prostitution, although proscribed by the Church, was regarded as preferable to the greater evils of rape, sodomy and masturbation. The tide of tolerance turned at the time of the Protestant reformation. In 18th century France, regulation started and prostitutes were given medical checks and licensed premises. In the early part of the 20th century, prostitution became illegal in America, but as with many other countries it has continued regardless.

'The pleasure is momentary, the position ridiculous, and the expense damnable.' Lord Chesterfield on prostitution

Mata Hari

Dutch girl Margaretha Zelle (1876–1917) adopted the stage name which she first used as an erotic dancer at the beginning of the 20th century. Her beauty and semi-naked appearances in Paris and Berlin earned her many fans and lovers, including soldiers from both sides in WWI. Her dealings and passing of monies led to allegations by MI5 that she was a double agent, resulting in her execution. The case was never proven: the free-living femme fatale had told the authorities that she did take money from German soldiers, but that it was not for passing them sensitive military information.

'There's so much damn porn, I never get out of the house.'
Jack Nicholson

PIMPING

Pimps are also known as macks, fancy men, panders, ponces and procurers. In the US, an established pimp is a 'player'; someone who uses violence and intimidation to control prostitutes is a guerrilla pimp; a man who employs psychological tricks to hook girls is a finesse pimp; new pimps are known as popcorn pimps, wannabes and hustlers. In the US, one third to two-thirds of prostitutes enter the profession by the age of 16: 90 per cent are physically abused and 80 per cent sexually abused by pimps, who expect them to earn $500 each day, providing their controllers with a generous yearly income approaching $200,000 per girl. The Players' Ball is held annually in Chicago to celebrate pimping. Tickets are $300.

Famous pimps: *Iceberg Slim, Charles Manson, Al Capone, Lucky Luciano*

'The big difference between sex for money and sex for free is that sex for money usually costs a lot less.' Brendan Behan

FATHER OF MODERN PORNOGRAPHY

Pietro Aretino (1492–1556) caused a sensation in Italy with his bold satirical book *Sixteen Postures* describing sexual positions. It was wildly erotic for the time and, with illustrations to match the lusty content by Giuliano Romano, it sealed Aretino's reputation as the smuttiest, most outrageously witty writer the Renaissance had seen. Casanova wrote in his memoirs of trying out the 'straight tree' position with a nun.

Eugène Pirou

This French photographer and filmmaker (1841–1909) was a pioneer of the blue or 'stag' movie, making more than 50 pornographic films in just one year. His 1896 debut *Le Coucher de la Marie*, which at three minutes was longer than the average film of the time, was a big hit in Paris. It inspired the beginning of a new genre, with fellow filmmakers Georges Méliès and Charles Pathé soon getting in on the act.

PENTHOUSE

Founded by painter Bob Guccione, this is the middle mag between the prettier *Playboy* and the lewder *Hustler*. Over time, it has changed its style from soft focus close-ups of the female anatomy plus touches of activity to explicit pictures of penetration, then moved on to a more sophisticated approach with fashion photographers and political features and a return to its soft roots, away from hardcore imagery. In 1984 its 15th anniversary September issue featured Vanessa Williams on the cover with George Burns and this was one of the biggest-selling magazines ever. The issue also became infamous with the discovery of the age of Traci Lords who was only 15 at the time: it is apparently illegal to own a copy with her centrefold appearance intact.

Quickies

* Fornication is from the Latin *fornix* for archway. In ancient Rome, prostitutes conducted their business under the Coliseum arches.

* US porn stars agreed to be tested for STDs every two weeks after HIV struck more than 60 of them in 2004.

* A telephone hustler is someone who leaves cards advertising sex in toilets and phone booths (see below).

* There are about 4.2 million Internet porn sites, with about 200 new ones added each day.

* In Japan vaginal prostitution is against the law, while fellatio for money is not.

* Recent reports suggest that 79 per cent of prostitutes in the Netherlands want to quit.

* In 2005, the Playboy Boutique was recognized as one of the top 40 retail successes in the world.

* A study in Colorado Springs found the average number of male customers to be 868 per working year per prostitute.

* Sex Industry unions around the world include COYOTE (call off your old tired ethics) in the US, and the Scarlet Alliance in Australia.

* Prostitution was common in the ancient world, including Israel, despite being forbidden under Jewish law.

* Roman poet Ovid (43BC–AD17) was the first to write pornography, including techniques on the best ways to get pleasure.

* There are an estimated 80,000 sex workers plying their trade in Britain today.

* There are three times as many adult bookstores and video outlets in America as there are McDonald's.

Calling Cards

In 1984, the repeal of the law that banned advertising from phone boxes led to their use by prostitutes to publicize their services. An estimated 13 million cards are placed in London's 700 phone boxes every year, from some 250 prostitutes. UK telecoms company BT claims it removes about 150,000 cards every week.

WORLD OF SEX

❖ *In 1999, Sweden's 'peace for women' legislation was the first of its kind in Europe, criminalizing the buying of sex on the streets, in clubs and massage parlours, but decriminalizing its sale. Jail sentences for clients range from six months to six years, while attempts to buy services can bring fines. The law recognizes prostitution as exploitation of women. Since its inception, there has been a dramatic fall-off in trade.*

❖ Thailand has a long tradition of prostitution, which came to world attention during the Vietnam War, and which is now worth $27 billion a year in foreign exchange. Estimates say up to 95 per cent of Thai men over 21 have visited prostitutes, and at least 450,000 Thai men visit brothels every day. Even though prostitution is largely condoned, custom strictly forbids pre-marital sex between dating couples. Although Bangkok is the unofficial sex capital of the world, prostitution was banned in Thailand in 1969.

❖ *Japan likewise has a long history of tolerating prostitution. The 1956 law banning it does not describe penalties, nor does it proscribe oral or anal sex.*

The estimated 3,500 sex businesses operating in one area of Tokyo offer such services as 'soaplands', 'image clubs' and 'pink salons'. More than 150,000 foreign women – Thai, Filipino and Russian mainly – work in the sex industry in Japan.

❖ In 2007, Argentinean prostitutes marched in Buenos Aires to promote awareness of their lives. The campaign was illustrated by a message on a statue in Mercy Park, also known as Prostitute Park, which declared: 'No woman is born a prostitute.'

❖ *Amsterdam's red light district is now home to a monument to celebrate prostitution around the world. 'Belle' designed by Els Rijerse was the idea of Mariska Majoor of the Prostitution Information Centre, a former prostitute herself. The bronze statue features a woman standing in a doorway with her hands on her hips.*

❖ Germany makes about $18 billion a year through its sex industry. The biggest growth in the online porn market is from the UK and a recent study revealed more users in the UK search 'porn' than any other English-speaking country.

THE MAIN ATTRACTION

'Sex is an emotion in motion.' Mae West

Sex in the movies has been around since pictures first moved. Through censorship and revolution, it has always managed to find its way on to the screen via audience imagination, metaphor, nudity and sound effects – sometimes it's even been the real thing. And that's not including pornography.

UNSIMULATED SEX IN FILM

Films using real sex are not labelled pornography if they have 'higher artistic intentions'. Mainstream films with real sex scenes include:

Dom Kallar oss Mods (1968) ✦ *Sweet Score* (1972) ✦ *The Image* (1975) ✦ *Through the Looking Glass* (1976) ✦ *Une vraie jeune fille* (1976) ✦ *Ai No Corrida* (1976) ✦ *Caligula* (1979) ✦ *Spetters* (1980) ✦ *Camping Cosmos* (1996) ✦ *Baise-Moi* (2000) ✦ *O Fantasma* (2000) ✦ *The Atrocity Exhibition* (2000) ✦ *Hundstage* (2001) ✦ *Intimacy* (2001) ✦ *Ken Park* (2002) ✦ *9 Songs* (2004) ✦ *All About Anna* (2005) ✦ *Batalla en el Cielo* (2005) ✦ *Inside Deep Throat* (2005) ✦ *8mm 2* (2005) ✦ *Shortbus* (2006) ✦ *Destricted* (2006)

THE LINES

'It's turkey time... gobble, gobble.' Gigli *(2003)* ✳ *'What is a sex crime?'* *'Not getting any.'* Wild Things *(1998)* ✳ *'Try the cock, Albert. It's a delicacy and you know where it's been.'* The Cook, the Thief, His Wife and Her Lover *(1989)* ✳ *'Go, get the butter.'* Last Tango in Paris *(1972)* ✳ *'I'm sorry, I can't, something big's come up.'* Goldfinger *(1964)* ✳ *'So, Jack tells me you've got a great big cock.'* Boogie Nights *(1997)*

Quickies

❋ Breathing caused Jayne Mansfield to pop out of her dress at the 1957 Oscars.

❋ In 2003, *Premiere* magazine's hottest sex scene ever came from *Blow-Up* (1966), where David Hemmings as the playboy photographer takes part in more than a photo shoot with supermodel Veruschka.

❋ Hugh Hefner bought the plot next to Marilyn Monroe in Los Angeles' Westwood Cemetery.

❋ In 2003, Playboy TV named Halle Berry and Billy Bob Thornton in *Monster's Ball* (2001) as its number one sexy scene.

❋ Despite being the biggest sex symbol the world has seen, and in the wake of three husbands and many lovers, Marilyn Monroe confessed to a friend that she had never had an orgasm.

❋ Jude Law was voted Sexiest Bottom by Odeon cinemas in 2005 for the bath scene in *The Talented Mr Ripley* (1999).

❋ Matthew McConaughey was named the most desirable New Year's Eve date in 2006 by OxiClean; he was also once found by police drumming his bongos in the nude.

❋ In 2003, *Empire* magazine named the *Out of Sight* (1998) moment where George Clooney and Jennifer Lopez are locked in the boot of a car as film's steamiest sex-free moment.

❋ *Pam & Tommy Lee: Hardcore & Uncensored* is the biggest-selling adult movie ever.

❋ The sexiest lips in the world belong to Angelina Jolie according to a poll in *FHM* in 2006.

❋ In 2000, *Maxim* magazine's greatest movie sex scene came from *Color of Night* (director's cut 1994), where Jane March and Bruce Willis enjoy time at home cooking steak, taking a shower and making the bed... shake.

❋ *Borat!: Cultural Learnings of America for Make Benefit Glorious Nation of Kazakhstan* is the first non-pornographic movie to be banned in Russia since the fall of the Soviet Union.

'Why do films not show sex? So many films are love stories, so why not show a love story through two people making love? It seems perverse.' Michael Winterbottom, director *9 Songs*

SEXY SCENES

The role of Frank in David Lynch's award-winning thriller *Blue Velvet* (1986) was too depraved for some actors, but it was grabbed with both hands and an oxygen mask by Dennis Hopper, who reportedly said, 'I've got to play Frank. Because I am Frank!' When the film came out, nuns from actress Isabella Rossellini's old convent school in Rome held masses to save her soul.

❖ 'The movie too HOT for words' – Billy Wilder's radical comedy *Some Like It Hot* (1959) touches on just about every sexual theme possible, from trans-sexuality and androgyny to sex appeal and impotence, including Tony Curtis and Marilyn Monroe's steamy glasses-kissing scene and Jack Lemmon and Joe E Brown's perverse tango. ❖ Sony Ericsson's sexiest film moment of all time – and one of the most played-back scenes ever – is Sharon Stone's leg-crossing moment in *Basic Instinct* (1992).

CHANNEL 4'S SEXIEST MOMENT

Dr No (1962) In 2003, the UK channel viewers' poll named the scene that inspired the massive popularity of the bikini and secured the success of the most famous and sexiest spy in the world: Ursula Andress surfacing from the sea as Honey Ryder made quite an impression on Sean Connery's Bond as well as the audience.

Top 10 Sexiest Movie Scenes

① *Secretary* (2002) James Spader spanking Maggie Gyllenhaal
② *Brokeback Mountain* (2005) Jake Gyllenhaal and Heath Ledger kissing
③ *Out of Sight* (1998) George Clooney and Jennifer Lopez in the trunk
④ *Betty Blue* (1986) Beatrice Dalle and Gean-Hughes Anglade's opening scene **⑤** *Cruel Intentions* (1999) Selma Blair and Sarah Michelle Gellar kissing **⑥** *Wild Things* (1998) Neve Campbell and Denise Richards washing the car **⑦** *Rear Window* (1954) Grace Kelly waking James Stewart with a kiss **⑧** *The Fabulous Baker Boys* (1989) Michelle Pfeiffer singing 'Makin' Whoopee' on the piano **⑨** *Mulholland Drive* (2001) Naomi Watts and Laura Harring sharing a bed **⑩** *The Hunger* (1983) Vampire seduction with Catherine Deneuve and Susan Sarandon   Source: LoveFilm 2006

THE ICONS

◆ Rodolfo Alfonzo Raffaelo Pierre Filibert Guglielmi di Valentina d'Antonguolla (1895–1926) was a gigolo in New York before becoming Hollywood's original male sex symbol Rudolph Valentino. His films, particularly *The Sheik*, had fans fainting at the sight of their idol, whose sex appeal induced a sexual frenzy never seen before. Jailed for bigamy and with women on the side, The Great Lover's premature death (from a perforated ulcer) caused worldwide hysteria, with riots at his funeral and devotees reportedly committing suicide.

◆ When Norma Jeane Mortenson became Marilyn Monroe (1926–1962), sex was to play the biggest role in her life. From casting couch horrors to her relationship with the US President, her trademark was her sex appeal: platinum hair, breathy voice, she moved like 'Jell-O on springs' and, in 1953, she appeared in the first edition of *Playboy* as its Sweetheart of the Month. In 1953, she was Advertising Association of the West's Most Advertised Girl in the World; in 1995, she was voted *Empire's* No.1 Sexiest Female Movie Star of All Time; in 1999, she was *Playboy's* No.1 Sex Star of the 20th Century; and in 2000, she was listed in *Time's* 100 Most Influential People of the 20th Century.

ALTERNATIVE SEX SYMBOLS

In Woody Allen's 1973 film Sleeper, *the orgasmatron, elevator-cum-vibrator technology, provides an otherwise incapable future population with orgasms.* ✷ *Orry-Kelly's eternally astounding near-transparent creation worn by Marilyn Monroe in the last act of* Some Like It Hot *won the Best Costume Design Oscar.* ✷ *In 9½ Weeks, the fridge provides one of the greatest cinematic examples of the relationship between food and sex.*

Russ Meyer

The King of the Nudies was a glamour photographer in the first years of *Playboy*, shooting centrefolds including his wife Eve. Following the success of *The Immoral Mr Teas* (1959), his reign in grindhouse theatres was cemented in the 1960s through the 1970s with the biggest boobs and the sleaziest satire in sexploitation, such as skin flicks *Faster, Pussycat! Kill! Kill!* (1965), *Mondo Topless* (1966), *Vixen!* (1968), *Blacksnake* (1973) and *Supervixens* (1975).

NOT SO SEXY SCENES

Showgirls *(1995) is the impressive recipient of an all-time Razzie record, with 13 nominations of dishonour and seven humiliating wins at the 1995 16th Golden Raspberry Awards. Paul Verhoeven was the first director to actually collect his award in person.* ☺ Basic Instinct
2 *(2006), aka* Basically, It Stinks, *picked up four awards and three nominations making it the 2007 Razzies' outright winner.* ☺ Shanghai Surprise *(1986) won a Razzie for Madonna's performance, which didn't put her off trying again in* Body of Evidence *(1993) and* Swept Away *(2002), for which she received further awards and nominations, all for the wrong reasons, including Worst Sex Scenes and Worst Movies.*

WORST SEX SCENES EVER

Empire magazine's survey compared the pool scene in *Showgirls*, intended as the 'best sex scene in the world', to 'the first 10 minutes of *Jaws*'. *Showgirls* also made number two in Guardian Unlimited's 2003 list, where 'humping like dolphins' was apparently not as bad as victor *Matrix Reloaded's* seemingly impossible mission that 'takes forever'.

TOP 10

1 Showgirls *(1995) Elizabeth Berkley and Kyle MacLachlan* # **2** Damage *(1992) Jeremy Irons and Juliette Binoche* # **3** Killing Me Softly *(2002) Heather Graham and Joseph Fiennes* # **4** Body of Evidence *(1993) Madonna and Willem Dafoe* # **5** Crimes of Passion *(1984) Kathleen Turner* # **6** The Specialist *(1994) Sharon Stone and Sly Stallone* # **7** Gigli *(2003) Ben Affleck and Jennifer Lopez* # **8** 40 Days and 40 Nights *(2003) Matt Sullivan and Shannyn Sossamon* # **9** Matrix Reloaded *(2003) Keanu Reeves and Carrie-Anne Moss* # **10** The Stud *(1978) Joan Collins and Oliver Tobias* Source: *Empire* 2005

Terms for sex films

Originally, they were called 'Smokers' because of the fug of smoke from chain-smoking, men-only audiences; by the 1950s, it was 'Stags' when screenings were still 100 per cent male; 'Nudies' were sex films of the 1960s; 'Sexploitation' was low-budget sex from the 1970s and 1980s; 'Soft core' with its high production values was for mainstream audiences; 'Porno' consists of Gonzo (without a plot) and Feature (very weak plot).

What you learn from porn videos: **1** Women wear high heels to bed **2** Men are never impotent **3** Women enjoy sex with ugly, middle-aged men **4** People in the 70s couldn't fuck without a wild guitar solo in the background **5** Women never have headaches/periods Source: debonairblog.com

Firsts on Film

DATE	TITLE	FIRST
1896	Le Coucher de la Marie	*Striptease, performed by Louise Willy*
1896	Fatima's Coochee-Coochee Dance	*Scene censorship, Fatima the belly dancer's gyrating pelvis was deemed too risqué*
1896	The Mary Irwin Kiss	*Kiss, performed by Mary Irwin and John Rice*
1909	To the Ecu of Gold	*Pornographic film*
1912	Dante's Inferno	*Full-frontal male nudity (the next wouldn't be until 1969)*
1916	A Daughter of the Gods	*Fully nude scene by a major star, Australian actress and professional swimmer Annette Kellerman*
1919	Anders als die Anderen	*Representation of homosexuality, with Conrad Veidt and Fritz Schulz*
1919	Back to God's Country	*Major female full-frontal nudity, Nell Shipman*
1921	The Sheik	*First male sex symbol, Rudolph Valentino*
1927	Flesh and the Devil	*French kiss (open mouth), performed by Greta Garbo and John Gilbert*
1929	Pandora's Box	*Fully developed lesbian character, Alice Roberts*
1931	Mädchen in Uniform	*Forbidden lesbian love, with Hertha Thiele and Dorothea Wieck*
1954	The Garden of Eden	*Naturist film in colour*
1959	The Immoral Mr Teas	*Non-naturist 'skin-flick', from cult director Russ Meyer, which also broke adult box office records*
1961	Victim	*Gay hero, Dirk Bogarde*
1963	Goldilocks and the Three Bears	*Nudist musical*

1963	Promises! Promises!	*Mainstream actress to appear nude in an American film, a topless Jayne Mansfield*
1964	The Pawnbroker	*Production Code seal granted to the view of a naked woman from the waist up*
1966	Blow-Up	*British feature film with full-frontal female nudity and first momentary view of pubic hair*
1968	The Killing of Sister George	*Genuine lesbian love scene in a mainstream film*
1969	Medium Cool	*Male and female nudity in an American mainstream film*
1969	Women in Love	*Full male nudity in a mainstream film, during the homoerotic scene between Oliver Reed and Alan Bates*
1970	The Boys in the Band	*Hollywood depiction of homosexual culture*
1970	The Stewardess	*Soft-core and most profitable 3D film*
1972	Fritz the Cat	*X-rated animated film*
1972	Last Tango in Paris	*Prosecution under the British Obscene Publications Act*
1978	National Lampoon's Animal House	*Major sex comedy aimed at teens and college kids, featuring Kevin Bacon and John Belushi*
1979	Caligula	*Hollywood sexploitation blockbuster, at a cost of $15m*
1985	Kiss of the Spider Woman	*Best Actor Oscar for a gay role, won by William Hurt*
1986	Desert Hearts	*Full-length lesbian feature written and directed by a woman, Donna Deitch*
1993	Philadelphia	*Major Hollywood film to focus on the subject of AIDS. Tom Hanks won Best Actor Oscar*
1999	Romance	*Erect penis in a mainstream film*
2005	Brokeback Mountain	*Mainstream gay/bi film, starring Jake Gyllenhaal and Heath Ledger, winning three Oscars*

SEXY BEASTS

Just like humans, the animal kingdom is not only about procreation but recreation, including hetero- and homosexuality, monogamy and promiscuity, masturbation, arousal, love and aggression, intersex and transgender.

'I would do anything Tim [Burton] wanted me to.
You know – have sex with an aardvark. I would do it.' Johnny Depp

Birds and the bees
Zoophilia comes from the Greek for humans sexually attracted to animals, while bestiality refers to sexual activity. ✤ The male bedbug has to drill an opening into the female using his curved penis. ✤ The prairie vole is monogamous, unusual in animals. ✤ Some lions mate more than 50 times a day. ✤ The pig's corkscrew-shaped penis can provide orgasms that last for 30 minutes. ✤ About every tenth black-headed gull couple is lesbian. ✤ Some species are both sexual and asexual. ✤ Turkeys can reproduce without having sex – this is called parthenogenesis. ✤ Snakes have two sex organs.
✤ Some mammals have an erectile bone. ✤ Orang-utans make dildos out of bark and wood. ✤ The walrus's penis is the longest of any living mammal and reaches up to 30 inches.

Some US zoos hold sex tours on Valentine's Day, providing champagne and uplifting stories of the inmates' lovemaking.
♦♦♦

Denmark and Norway have no bestiality laws. As long as the animals are not harmed, it is legal for humans to engage in sex with them at bordellos. One farmer said he was surprised by the distance his customers travelled to hook up with his animals.

WILD THINGS

❖In May 2007, a hen in India was reported to have experienced a gradual and spontaneous sex change into a cockerel. The University of Florida's Institute of Food and Agricultural Sciences confirmed this rare phenomenon is possible.

❖A study into nature reserves in Ghana, which came out in 2003, showed that monogamous species are more likely to die out than those with harems.

❖Bisexual male bottlenose dolphins use the nose to simulate oral sex; a quarter of swans are raised by male couples and chase the female away once she has laid the egg; female bonobo monkeys rub genitals against each other; and male giraffes have orgies.

❖Some animals experience external fertilization, such as most fish: the female lays her eggs, which are then sprayed by the male.

❖Dominant female spotted hyenas have many male partners, which have to penetrate the clitoris, which grows seven inches out of the body like a penis. It has a one-inch diameter birth canal for giving birth to a two-pound cub.

❖Female fireflies choose male partners by their flash patterns. A long flash means more sperm, which means more eggs.

❖One cabbage aphid, in ideal conditions of food and safety, could give rise to 41 generations of offspring in one season: one and a half billion billion billion aphids, three times the weight of all humans.

❖The entire male population of the brown antechinus, an Australian marsupial mouse, spends two weeks of the year having sex with as many females as possible, then dies from the stress of the chase.

'As she lay there dozing next to me, one voice inside my head kept saying, "Relax, you are not the first doctor to sleep with one of his patients," but another kept reminding me, "Howard, you are a veterinarian."' Roger Matthews

MYTHS

Some people love to tell sex stories of incredible feats. And some people will believe anything...

TOP URBAN LEGENDS

✳ One particular true story of 'the couple who have to call for help during a sex game' has surfaced too often to be convincing: rescuers find the woman naked and handcuffed to the bed and her partner/husband unconscious and dressed as Batman, having apparently been role-playing at 'rescuing' her, but having knocked himself out on the ceiling fan instead.

✳ Despite its role in *Braveheart*, the medieval practice of *jus primae noctis* – or noblemen claiming the right to bed peasant brides on their wedding nights – is backed up by little or no supporting evidence.

✳ Also declared untrue was the tale of the model and former cheerleader who took a pharmacist to court after she bought spermicidal jelly from the store, but became pregnant anyway even though she had put the product on her toast and eaten it...

✳ The gerbil is innocent. The old tale of the A&E dash to retrieve a gerbil from the rectum of an imaginative fan of sex toys also appears to be a fantasy. Genuine 'foreign bodies', however, recovered by nimble-fingered nurses (or surgeons) include vibrators, glass bottles, deodorant bottles, carrots, pencils, pieces of frozen chicken and table legs.

✳ Although the Space Shuttle does take its astronauts to places most have never been, according to NASA, the earth hasn't moved for them and no sex experiments in space have yet taken place. Allegedly!

✳ It's true. The excuse for eating chocolate

for 'pleasure' has been destroyed and Casanova can put down his libido to a natural talent and not his pre-conquest dose of hot chocolate. Phenylethylamine, which provides feelings of attraction, love and euphoria, is found in chocolate. However, sadly, recent studies have revealed that the majority of the 'love chemical' is already broken down before it can reach the brain.

✳ Drinking fizzy drinks doesn't prevent pregnancy. The colouring agent Yellow No.5 is not a contraceptive and has been judged safe by the FDA, so, while using sodas as spermicidal douches and contraceptives is not recommended they are best used to wash down the real thing.

✳ Using two condoms at the same time will not provide double protection. All double-bagging does is increase the chance of the condoms splitting.

✳ Catherine the Great did have a passion for her horses – but not in the biblical sense. Her death was not the result of being crushed under the weight of her latest equine lover; it was from natural causes, in bed, no horse.

✳ Despite fuelling rumours that the cops had caught Mick Jagger 'enjoying' an intimate Mars Bar from between her legs by apparently appearing in the brand's commercial with the slogan 'Pleasure you can't measure', Marianne Faithfull has been firm in her denial that the event ever happened.

A man was very, very late home one night, so to please his wife, before she had time to get upset, he decided to surprise her with great sex. After the amazing event, he went downstairs to get himself a self-congratulatory drink for his inspiration. 'Ssshhh!' said a voice from the living room sofa. 'Your mother's visiting. Don't wake her, she's asleep in our bed.'

SEX AND RELIGION

'Good girls go to heaven, bad girls go everywhere.' Mae West

Death of a Catholic cliché

November 2004: the Vatican publishes *It's A Sin Not To Do It*, a booklet redrawing the boundaries of permissible sex for Catholics, largely in response to the falling birthrate among Roman Catholics in Italy. The intention was to show that sex and the Church is not all warnings and taboos and that it was time to focus on the positive. Forty years earlier, the previous Vatican treatise on sexual behaviour taught that even French kissing between unmarried couples was sinful.

'I trained to be a priest – started to. I went to seminary school when I was 11. I wanted to be a priest, but when they told me I could never have sex, not even on my birthday, I changed my mind.'
Johnny Vegas, comedian

CATHOLIC TASTES

✝Pope John XII (955–964) turned Laterno's Basilica di San Giovanni into a brothel.

✝A woman called Joan, who had disguised herself as a monk, is said to have become Pope around 1100. In time, she fell pregnant, but gave birth to her child during an Easter parade in Rome and was stoned to death by the crowd. Thereafter, popes had to face the public gaze in a special chair – with a hole in the base through which a cardinal could check they had testicles.

✝Pope Alexander VI (1492–1503) participated in an orgy, organized by his son Don Cesare Borgia, attended by 50 courtesans and prostitutes who danced naked before picking up chestnuts from the floor as everyone watched. Prizes were then given to the men with the highest number of sexual conquests.

✠Pilgrims visiting the Sanctuary of Fatima in Portugal were given free maps of the shrine, featuring the image of the Virgin Mary, but when they turned them over, they were shocked to find sex toys and aphrodisiacs advertised on the other side.

✠A popular Californian Christian radio station surprised its listeners in 2006 when, instead of spiritual voices and songs of praise, they heard carnal moans and groans and sexually explicit songs. Apparently the station's new owner was just giving them a wake-up call on his arrival.

✠In 2006, a German church group in Nuremburg produced a calendar with a modern take on Bible scenes, including Adam and Eve and the dance of Salome. The difference was the models were naked. Despite controversy, further copies have been printed to meet demand.

✠Dr Heba Kotb, a Cairo-born sex therapist broadcaster and writer across the Muslim world, tells her audience to have and enjoy sex as much as they can, all in accordance with the writings of the Koran.

✠The reverend John McQueen scandalized Edinburgh in the 1600s when he became so obsessed with the gorgeous Mrs Euphame Scott that he stole her undergarments from the washing line and had them made up into a waistcoat and trousers .

'I thank God I was raised Catholic, so sex will always be dirty.'
John Waters, film maker

✳

'They'd been in the folk mass choir when they were in school but that hadn't really been singing. Jimmy said real music was sex... they were starting to agree with him. And there wasn't much sex in 'Morning Has Broken' or 'The Lord Is My Shepherd'.'
From *The Commitments* by Roddy Doyle (1987)

THE ART OF SEX

THE SEX OF ART

Love and promiscuity have always been associated with creativity. From bohemian passions to obsessions with muses, sex has been a behind-the-scenes inspiration as well the subject of many masterpieces throughout the history of art.

PRELIMINARY SKETCHES

✎ When studying ancient sculptures, art psychologist IC McManus discovered that 51 per cent show the left testicle as lower, 22 per cent the right as lower and 27 per cent level

✎ Yves Klein made his female models smear paint on their naked bodies and make art by imprinting themselves on paper

✎ Leonardo da Vinci is said to have thought the lungs had canals leading to the sexual organs and to have invented high heels

✎ Jeff Koons' 'Made In Heaven' series depicts him in a number of explicit sexual positions with his then wife, ex-porn star/politician *La Cicciolina*, now Ilona Staller

✎ When Michelangelo's *David* was lent to London in 1857, a two-foot-high fig leaf was placed in front of his genitals to prevent shocking Queen Victoria

✎ In a *Simpsons* episode, Homer is embarrassed when he takes home a Robert Mapplethorpe book of ultra-risqué photographs by mistake

✎ Agalmatophilia, also known as Pygmalionism, is sexual attraction to statues, dolls and mannequins

---

'I have always wanted a mistress who was fat, and I have never found one. To make a fool of me, they are always pregnant.'
Paul Gauguin, 1848–1903

Creativity = Sex

Research by psychologists at the University of Newcastle-upon-Tyne and the Open University in England revealed in 2005 that both male and female creative geniuses were likely to have twice as many partners as other men and women. The study showed that the more work the artist produced, the more sexual activity they engaged in.

'It is your work in life that is the ultimate seduction.'
Pablo Picasso, 1881–1973

✳

'Only love interests me, and I am only in contact with things that revolve around love.'
Marc Chagall, 1887–1985

✳

'Sex is more exciting on the screen and between the pages than between the sheets.' Andy Warhol, 1928–1987

'Art is vice. You don't marry it legitimately, you rape it.'
Edgar Degas, 1834–1917

✳

'Body experience… is the centre of creation.'
Barbara Hepworth, 1903–1975

✳

'Love always brings difficulties, that is true, but the good side of it is that it gives energy'
Vincent van Gogh, 1853–1890

La Gioconda

Is she or isn't she? Regarded as one of the most seductive figures in history, Leonardo da Vinci's painting of the 'Mona Lisa' has caused many viewers to try to read her 'smile'. Interpretations include pregnancy, 'she's got facial paralysis' and, according to a computer at the University of Amsterdam in 2006, she's 83 per cent happy, 9 per cent disgusted, 6 per cent fearful and 2 per cent angry. Freud thought her smile represented Leonardo's erotic obsession with his mother and, to ensure La Gioconda's ongoing association with sex, she's even appeared on a condom packet.

LIVES AND TIMES

➤CARAVAGGIO 1571–1610 His works are filled with sexual references and semi-naked boys; he often used prostitutes to pose for him, but is believed to have had a preference for men. He once had to flee Rome after killing a young man in a brawl and was allegedly chased by the Grand Master of the Knights of Malta for sleeping with his favourite page.

➤PAUL GAUGUIN 1848–1903 He left his family and was drawn to live in Tahiti, seeing it as an erotic paradise where he could have as much sex as he could handle, which included questionable relationships with younger island girls.

➤VINCENT VAN GOGH 1853–1890 He had a relationship with model and prostitute Sien Hoomik. In 1888, suffering from mental illness, he cut off his ear and gave it to a prostitute as a gift.

➤HENRI DE TOULOUSE-LAUTREC 1864–1901 He produced pictures of bordellos and clubs, particularly of dancing girls at the Moulin Rouge and lesbian scenes of the decadent district of Montmartre. Rumoured to have caught syphilis from Rosa la Rouge who lived in a brothel.

➤PABLO PICASSO, 1881–1973 His sex life was as prolific as his art; he had two wives and a considerable number of partners and mistresses. Prostitutes were often the subject of his Blue Period. 'Nude in a Black Armchair' sold for $45.1 million at Christie's in 1999, the fourth-highest price paid for a Picasso. Long-time lover Françoise Gilot left him because of his constant affairs – he was in his 80s.

➤EGON SCHIELE 1890–1918 Was passionate about sex and had many mistresses. He was accused of obscenity: his nude paintings caused scandals; he had teenagers pose for him and was sent to jail for seducing an under-age girl. Some self-portraits included an erection.

➤SALVADOR DALI 1904–1989 'Le Grand Masturbateur' (1929) and 'Espectro del Sex-Appeal' (1932) are said to represent his fear of sex. He had a rumoured homosexual affair with Spanish writer friend Lorca. In 1928, he went to Paris and asked a cab driver for a good brothel. Fell completely in love with

Russian surrealist Gala, wooed her by waxing his armpit and dying it blue; she became his muse and lover.
➤ FRIDA KAHLO 1907–1954 Her husband Diego Rivera said she 'breaks all the taboos of the woman's body and of female sexuality'. Maintained a lively and fiery sex life, including lesbian liaisons and an affair with Leon Trotsky.

➤ GILBERT AND GEORGE 1943– and 1942– Living works of art and living together, they are presumed lovers by many but never answer questions about their sex lives. Their sexual images address taboos, using sperm and other human secretions; their works include 'Bum Holes', 'Sperm Eaters' 'Naked Forest' and 'Naked Shit Pictures'.

Turner's Erotica

The 19th century art critic John Ruskin was so devastated when he discovered the content of his idol JMW Turner's (1775–1851) saucy sketchbooks that he pretended to burn them so no one would witness what he saw as obscenities. The claim was recently questioned when, in 2004, Turner expert Ian Warrell of the Tate discovered a huge collection of the artist's drawings of a sexual nature, such as women's genitals and erotic poses and became certain Ruskin couldn't bring himself to burn them after all. As an illustration of Ruskin's prudery it has been rumoured, maybe in jest, that he did not consummate his marriage as he was repulsed by the sight of his bride's pubic hair.

'Love is when the desire to be desired takes you so badly that you feel you could die of it.' Henri de Toulouse-Lautrec, 1864–1901

✳

'I had many affairs, but I was never into quickie sex. I've only slept with maybe a thousand men.' Robert Mapplethorpe, 1946–1989

✳

'When I've painted a woman's bottom so that I want to touch it, then the painting is finished.' Pierre-Auguste Renoir, 1841–1919

NOW FOR SOMETHING COMPLETELY DIFFERENT...

All part of the service

A UK company is realizing fantasies of the perfect hired help and is providing men in teeny tiny aprons with athletic bodies, intelligence and charm. Butlers in the Buff specialists are booked for functions from birthdays to corporate events. Meanwhile, in California, a builder has been exposed more than once for working with no clothes on, justifying his state to surprised clients as less restricted therefore producing a better standard of work. And in Germany in 2006, to solve a shortage of nurses, about 30 prostitutes enrolled on training courses to become geriatric nurses, making use of their special talents in dealing with people.

There's more to the world of fetishism than shoes. Here, sexual desires and taste are highly individual and urges sometimes uncontrollable.

✳ ABASIOPHILIA *Sexual attraction to people with mobility facilitators, especially equipment such as braces or wheelchairs.*

✳ COPROPHILIA *Sexual excitement from the use of faeces, also known as Dirty Sanchez.*

✳ EMETOPHILIA *Sexual arousal from the act of vomiting, the individual's or their partner's.*

✽ HYBRISTOPHILIA *Sexual attraction to violent crime or criminals.*
✽ KLISMAPHILIA *Sexual pleasure from an enema.*
✽ MACROPHILIA *The taste for the demonstration of strength or muscular men or women.*

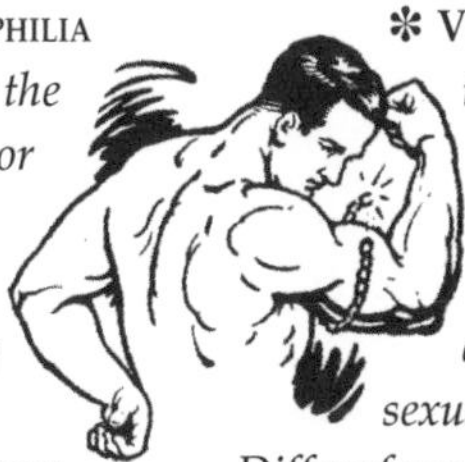

✽ NASOPHILIA *Arousal from the sight of, touching and sucking the nose.*

✽ NYOTAIMORI *A Japanese food fetishist practice of eating sushi off the body of a naked woman.*
✽ SOMNOPHILIA *Arousal from having sexual contact with a person who is asleep.*
✽ STHENOLAGNIA *The love of giant, overpowering women.*
✽ TERATOPHILIA *An attraction to deformed people or amputees.*
✽ TROILISM *The practice of one person watching two other people having sex.*
✽ UROLAGNIA *The desire to be urinated on. Allegedly, advocates of 'golden showers' included Rembrandt and Adolf Hitler. In New Zealand, it is illegal to publish anything depicting urolagnia and this can attract up to 10 years in prison.*
✽ VORAREPHILIA *The desire to be eaten alive or eat someone else or to watch.*
✽ ZOOPHILIA *An attraction to animals, sexually or otherwise. Differs from bestiality. Penetrative sexual activity with animals is illegal in the UK, the US, Canada and New Zealand; however it is legal in Sweden, Denmark and the Netherlands. In Peru it is illegal for an unmarried man to share his home with a female llama.*

'Is sex dirty? Only if it is done right.' Woody Allen

WAYS OF THE WORLD

'Continental people have sex life;
the English have hot-water bottles.'
George Mikes, *How To Be An Alien*, 1946

POMPEII

Architects discovered evidence indicating that sex in Roman times was an everyday part of life regardless of orientation or social standing. Common décor included walls covered with explicitly sexual frescos, gardens filled with representations of giant phalluses and brothels and taverns brimming with business. As a religious people, they saw sex as a gift from the gods, especially Venus and the Vestal Virgins who were honoured as divine, and phallic amulets featured in nearly every doorway to ward off evil. It was considered a scandal to expect a woman to sleep only with her husband, and same-sex liaisons were the norm. The only sexual taboo was the oral act which was seen as unclean, but sex was generally revered and respected until the emperors began to use it as a tool of power and then it became a battlefield.

In the line of duty

Following the 2006 Football World Cup, Germany discovered scoring had not been confined to the field of play when there was a much-needed baby boom nine months later. 'World Cup Babies' reversed the unwelcome downward trend in the country's birth rate. As role models, policewomen were targeted to get the ball rolling and given a €7 discount on herbal aphrodisiac Femi-X, the female equivalent of Viagra, plus a DVD of sex tips.

¿te hace un polvete? Fancy a quickie?

- Polynesians are systematically instructed on sexual techniques by their elders.
- In Japan, No-Pan Kissa coffee houses have mirrored floors to allow customers to look up waitresses' skirts. Its name translates simply as the 'No Panties Café'.
- In Santa Cruz, Bolivia, men are not allowed to have sex with mother and daughter – at the same time.
- Apparently, a man who is tripped during a Colombian dance by a Goajiro woman has to have sex with her.
- Greece was named officially as the sexiest country in the world, according to a 2005 Durex survey, with citizens enjoying sex 138 times a year – well over three times the global average.
- Saleswomen can legally trade topless in Liverpool, England – if they work in tropical fish stores.
- During the wedding ceremony, the Incas gave each other their sandals as an official symbol of marriage.
- Female islanders of Lesu in the Pacific show their genitals when they are attracted to a man.
- A Balanta tribe bride of Africa was married as long as her wedding dress lasted. For a quick split, she could rip the dress to shreds.
- In China and Taiwan, the expression 'wearing a green hat' applies to a man whose wife is unfaithful. Many Taipei post-office workers, therefore, whose uniform was completely green, were understandably reluctant to wear the hat that came with it.
- Tang Empress Wu Hou is said to have expected visitors to perform oral sex on her as a sign of respect.
- Cleopatra is thought to have made her diaphragm from camel faeces.
- In the US, 24 states allow impotence as solid grounds for divorce.

'One half of the world cannot understand the pleasures of the other.' Jane Austen

SEX ON LOCATION

Sex in unusual places provides that extra frisson...

AROUND THE WORLD

According to the Durex sex survey of 2005, 15 per cent of people questioned had had sex at work; Australians preferred the great outdoors, with 54 per cent having had sex in the park; 21 per cent of Americans and Canadians have done it in front of a camera; and for eight out of ten Italians passion was best found in the car.

DOWN THE LANE

In the Middle Ages, a streetwalker's patch was denoted by the name 'Gropec**t Lane' and streets of this name were located throughout Britain. Similarly themed byways include Love Lane, Fondle Street and Puppekirty Lane which translates from 'Poke Skirt Lane'. Stories that Horsleydown comes from 'Whores Lie Down' sadly seem untrue as it actually means somewhere horses could graze.

Naked weekend

Where do nudists book their holidays? The whitest sands and sunniest climes would be a stereotypical guess, but British Naturism booked its 2006 vacation at Alton Towers theme park in England – in November! Taking all the rooms and having the run of the rides in the off-season meant guests could take off their clothes and really make themselves at home... that's if their bits didn't fall off with the cold.

> *'Love in an elevator/Lovin' it up till I hit the ground.'*
> Aerosmith, 'Love in an Elevator', 1989

'Bed is the poor man's opera.' Italian proverb

TRANSPORT OF DELIGHT

In the golden days of Japanese prostitution, whores plied their trade on small boats. In the 10th century, *asobi* – the term comes from the verb 'to play' – included trained musicians, singing sirens who lured men aboard and charmed the money from their pockets. According to 12th-century poet Oe Masafusa, 'Their voices halt the clouds and their tones drift with the wind blowing over the water. Passers-by cannot help but forget their families.' According to another description of the time, the younger women melted men's hearts 'with rouge and powder and songs and smiles', while the older women carried parasols and poled the boats along. The 11th-century courtier Fujiwara Akihira praised one particular practitioner as follows: 'Her vigour in soliciting lovers, her knowledge of all the sexual positions, the merits of her lute strings and buds of wheat [genitalia], and her mastery of the dragon's flutter and tiger's tread techniques... all are her endowments.' By the late 12th century, a cold wind blew for the *asobi* and they were forced on to dry land, into the inns that lined the waterside and doubtless into the hands of pimps.

SEX UNDER THE STARS

In 1849, in the Paris cemeteries of Père Lachaise and Montparnasse, Sergeant François Bertrand started digging up corpses with his bare hands in order to have sex with them. A man with violent torture fantasies, he also liked biting into corpses and leaving toothmarks all over them. Bertrand was caught and convicted on 15 counts, but only served a year in jail. He committed suicide a year after his release.

Toothing was the 'hi-tech sex craze of 2007': strangers flirt with each other on Bluetooth and seek to have sex in unusual spots such as the toilets on a train.

STRANGERS ON A PLANE

Sex on a plane is the basic requirement to join the Mile High Club, a term used for couples who have achieved satisfaction in the sky. Famous members allegedly include Ralph Fiennes with attendant Lisa Robertson, marking their membership and the end of her role with Qantas on a flight from Darwin to Mumbai. A number of companies offer planes specially equipped for this purpose with champagne and a furnished cabin to help amorous passengers make their own in-flight entertainment and join the club. There is also an actual Mile High Club online platform for people to add their tales to the other knee-rubbing passengers' stories of quite saucy and heated moments since 1996. According to the club's site, the honour of being founder goes to Laurence Sperry, fittingly one of the inventors of the autopilot. When giving lessons to a Mrs Waldo Polk in 1916, the pair flew into trouble and the plane fell into the bay waters near New York. Rescuers discovered them safe and sound – and with their clothes in considerable disarray.

No brakes

A couple in Jerusalem were fined for having sex in their car. So? Not only were they so eager to satisfy their passion that they didn't pull over, but the road block they caused was in the fast lane.

> ### Eroticar
>
> A 2007 'Cars and Summer Romance Survey' by On Demand TV revealed that 70 per cent of Americans want to do it in the car during the summer, with nearly 30 per cent choosing a BMW, 24 per cent preferring a Mercedes and 30 per cent going for a Hummer as the vehicle of choice; 66 per cent would date someone because of their car. Amomaxia is the term for having sex in a parked car.

DOGGING

This is an activity gaining popularity in the UK. Enthusiasts meet at secluded locations either to watch other people having sex in cars, or to have sex in cars watched by other people. Depends on whether you are a Peeping Tom or an exhibitionist, and how you're feeling that day. Footballer Stan Collymore, who was in *Basic Instinct 2* with Sharon Stone, admitted going dogging a dozen or more times. The derivation of the term is disputed. It either comes from the idea of using an imaginary dog as an excuse to hang around the bushes, telling your wife you are taking the dog for a walk to hide your true intentions, or the thought of copulating in public like a canine. Those who oppose dogging, often genuine dog walkers, carry megaphones that make the sound of police sirens to frighten doggers away. The Ultimate Dogging Championship is supposedly held at Rivington, Lancashire. Events include the 10-Man Train, Pearly Rain and The Most Extreme Slapper.

'Why don't we do it in the road?/No one will be watching us.'
The Beatles, 'Why Don't We Do It in the Road?', 1968

Love and war

WAR AND SEX

When no one knows what the next day will bring, men and women tend to throw caution to the winds .

AMERICAN CIVIL WAR

During the war of 1861–1865, prostitution flourished near the army camps, providing soldiers with 'horizontal refreshment', as it was known. By 1862, Washington DC had roughly 450 brothels and some 7,500 full-time prostitutes. About 8 per cent of Union soldiers were treated for VD during the war.

WWI

The Conscription Act of 1917 forbade prostitution near army camps and whores were dubbed 'disease spreaders' as military bases became distribution points for STDs. WWI led to an epidemic of syphilis in the US, particularly among black Americans, that lasted 40 years. France, for example, had a high rate of VD and many of its citizens proved all too susceptible to the 'lure of khaki', passing on STDs to troops. Penicillin, the cure for syphilis, was not developed until the end of WWII.

Japan

Before, during and after WWII, the Japanese army procured over 200,000 'comfort women' – sex slaves from China, Korea and other occupied territories – forced to perform sexual services for the soldiers.

Famous 'Forces Sweethearts', WWII sex symbols who helped raise morale: Vera Lynn, Betty Grable, Gracie Fields, Marlene Dietrich, Anne Shelton

VIETNAM

In Vietnam, the US military dissuaded GIs from using local prostitutes by spreading rumours of 'black syphilis', leading to a lifetime of banishment and the sufferer being declared KIA (killed in action).

Non-lethal weapon

The Pentagon once contemplated developing a 'hormone bomb', releasing aphrodisiacs and chemicals supposed to turn enemy soldiers homosexual so they would be too attracted to each other to fight.

WWII

➤ The use of libido suppressants by the British, US and Russian armies in World War II, such as bromide in soldiers' tea and saltpetre in food, is now regarded as a myth. Sedatives with dangerous side-effects wouldn't appear to be the best thing to administer during a war. However, the US military did distribute roughly 50 million condoms every month and it also created two mobile VD treatment centres to chase its troops across Europe following D-Day.

➤ *American GIs in Australia and Britain were memorably described as 'overpaid, oversexed and over here' due to their confidence in courting the ladies – and their success rate. Sex out of wedlock and affairs were rife. The Baby Boom that followed produced about 50 million children between 1946 and 1961 and marked a huge increase in illegitimate births.*

➤ The Japanese, the Americans, the British and the Germans all bombarded their enemies with propaganda leaflets featuring graphic pornography in the hope of undermining them. The tactic was a failure. Rather than desert their stations, most soldiers kept the leaflets and used them as pin-ups. Soldiers even collected their own side's leaflets and traded them like baseball cards.

ACCIDENTS WILL HAPPEN

'Sexual intercourse is kicking death in the ass while singing.'
Charles Bukowski

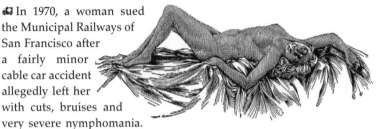

In 1970, a woman sued the Municipal Railways of San Francisco after a fairly minor cable car accident allegedly left her with cuts, bruises and very severe nymphomania. In the five years since the event, she had slept with more than 500 men: 10 of her lovers revealed she had been an easy conquest and psychologists blamed fear for causing her newfound urge. The jury took five minutes to find for her and award $50,000.

In 1988, in New York, a 34-year-old man was admitted to hospital with a permanent erection after injecting cocaine into his urethra, with the aim of heightening pleasure during sex. It ultimately led to gangrene which cost him nine fingers, both legs and his penis.

The dangerous act of masturbation with a vacuum cleaner is apparently not as rare as it should be and has landed many practitioners in hospital. Injuries include losing the glans penis.

Kenneth Pinyan, aka Mr Hands, of Seattle died of a perforated colon after submitting to anal intercourse with an Arab stallion called 'Bullseye', an act he had videotaped.

Asphyxiophilia – the practice of attempting to heighten orgasm by reducing the normal amount of oxygen and blood to the brain – has produced such notable casualties as Stephen Milligan, a Conservative MP, 1994, who was found dead in his London flat wearing stockings and suspenders with a piece of cord tied from his neck to his ankles – bizarrely, he had a segment of satsuma in his mouth (probably in a vain attempt to stop him passing out) – and possibly Michael Hutchence of INXS in 1997, whose death was officially given as suicide. The first recorded case of auto-erotic asphyxia was of Czech composer and double bassist Frantisek Kotzwara in 1791, who tied his neck with a ligature which was fastened to a doorknob and died having sex with a prostitute. She had refused his earlier request to cut off his testicles.

DEAD AND BURIED

☠ In ancient Rome, the *bustuariae* – grave-watchers – were specialized prostitutes who worked in cemeteries, some even taking their clients inside the tombs.

☠ In 1933, radiologist Carl Tanzer took his obsession with a dead patient to the extreme. Keeping her body in an above-ground tomb, he reconstructed her with plaster of Paris and clothed her. The woman's sister suspected him of necrophilia and eventually found her rather well-dressed, decomposed sibling in Tanzer's bed.

☠ *In delicato flagrante morto* – death during sex – has allegedly claimed notables such as the president of France, Félix Faure, in 1899, who apparently died of apoplexy while receiving oral sex in his office. Reports also point to one-time US vice president Nelson Rockefeller meeting his demise during the act with his 26-year-old research assistant in 1979.

THE CHASE

When it comes to attracting a partner, some people have a natural flair for flirting, while others have a natural fear. Then there are those with the confidence and the persistence – but no idea.

THE ONE

American sexologist John Money introduced the idea of the 'lovemap' in 1980. Triggers in the mind go off when people see something in someone they like. These triggers are set during youth, but can alter with age and experience. Lovemaps appear in the subconscious and are idealized erotic guides to Mr and Mrs Right – and to Mr and Mrs Wrong. Many researchers suggest choices resemble people's parents, strong characters from childhood or even themselves. The tendency is to pick partners with similar looks and intelligence; however, it is also the case that opposites attract as people seek attributes they lack or find exciting and new. Turn-ons reveal themselves via all the senses, initially blinding people to any flaws. That's love. And where 'love is blind' comes from.

Bar Code

Invented by Lilibet Foster and Lynn Fischer, 'Bar Code' is a sign language that allows the timid and tongue-tied to communicate with their hands, chat up potential dates and remain cool, calm and collected without the public humiliation of everyone else hearing you.

You know you've had a successful date when they ask, 'When will I see you again?'.

♦♦♦

If they reply, 'I'll call you,' you know when you haven't.

'Sex appeal is fifty per cent what you've got and fifty per cent what people think you've got.' Sophia Loren

FIRST IMPRESSIONS

A speed-dating study in Edinburgh, Scotland, in 2006 revealed that the chat-up lines with best results, including 'What's your favourite pizza topping?', were ones that demanded more than a yes or no answer. Most participants made up their minds about a person within 30 seconds of meeting. No pressure there then. In 2004, 'This time next year, let's be laughing together' was announced as the ultimate Japanese chat-up line.

FIVE TURN-ONS
Is it hot in here? Or is it you? ✱ *Screw me if I'm wrong, but you want to kiss me, don't you?* ✱ *I'd really like to see how you look when I'm naked.* ✱ *If we're going to regret this in the morning, we could sleep till the afternoon.* ✱ *Hi, I'm Mr/Miss Right, someone said you were looking for me.*

FIVE INSULTING COMPLIMENTS
I may not be the best-looking guy here, but I'm the only one talking to you. ✱ *You remind me of cheese. I like cheese.* ✱ *You have a bottom like an onion. It makes me want to cry.* ✱ *You're ugly, but you intrigue me.* ✱ *Do you mind if I stare at you close up rather than from across the room?*

FIVE TURN-OFFS
Before you say no, I'm not a freak. ✱ *Do you like to dance? Good, I want to talk to your friend.* ✱ *I'm not really tall, I'm standing on my wallet.* ✱ *Hey, bird, sit on my face and I'll guess your weight.* ✱ *I'd like to screw your brains out, but I guess someone beat me to it.*

Why Wait?
Sadie Hawkins Day, where girls take the lead and pursue the boys, originated in Al Capp's comic strip *L'il Abner*. Sadie's father set up a race where the unmarried women in town chased after available men.

SPORTING ROMPS

ON YOUR MARKS

The Spartans of ancient Greece were the most relaxed in their attitude to nudity and are thought to have been the first sportsmen to enter the Olympic games naked. They won many events and this encouraged the rest of the athletes to follow birthday suit. The word 'gymnasium' comes from the Greek *gymnos* for naked and the Greeks spent much of their time training in the nude to achieve bodies as perfect as their gods' – a tradition that was revived in the 90s by the Nude Olympics sponsored by the Canyon State Naturists in America. The games were revived in 1896, by which time naked sports were no longer the thing.

VILLAGE PEOPLE

US swimmer Nelson Diebel, who won two golds at Barcelona, told *Scotland on Sunday* the Olympic village is 'a two week-long private party for thousands of hard bodies'. When 10,000 athletes, pumped up and primed for action, come into close proximity – with a free internet service to help them 'hook up' – sparks fly. In Albertville, at the winter Olympics, the condom machines took just two hours to empty and had to be refilled round the clock. In Sydney, an initial 70,000 condoms were ordered for athletes and 20,000 more had to be ferried in (the Cubans were the first to get through their ration). Even then, protection ran out three days before the games were over. In Salt Lake City, 250,000 condoms were handed out despite the concerns of local Mormons. 'It's not an orgy,' said former alpine skiing champion Carrie Sheinberg, 'but it is socially vigorous.'

NO SEX BEFORE THE BIG EVENT

Muhammad Ali is said to have abstained from sex for six weeks before going into the ring because sex before a fight can affect performance. But recent research has suggested that a full recovery is possible only 10 hours after sexual activity. Some scientists have found that the effort used to make love is hardly enough to make a difference and it can even help reduce pain, while others have said that holding out could help concentration and giving in could use up the aggression so effective in some sports. However, Italian professor of endocrinology Emmanuelle A Jannini's studies revealed the opposite, that abstention actually decreases testosterone so a session of sexual intercourse before the game could have just the right result. Perhaps not, though. In the 1974 Football World Cup final, the Dutch team are said to have been advised to indulge the night before. They scored in the first minute of the game, whereas the Germans, who had been told to abstain, were rewarded with two late goals, taking them to victory. George Best, the footballing hero who famously always had a beautiful woman on his arm, apparently told British chat show host Michael Parkinson that he thought the closest to a game he'd had sex was half-time.

Olympic 'gender appraisals'

Stanislawa Walasiewicz, winner of gold in the 100 m at the LA Olympics in 1932, was discovered to possess 'male genitalia' after her death in 1980 ● Russian sisters Tamara and Irina Press, who broke 26 world records between them, failed to reappear in competition after sex tests started in 1966 ● Princess Anne was the sole female contestant to avoid a sex test at the 1976 Olympics
● Sex tests were discontinued in 1999

SPORTING PERFORMANCES

The most male orgasms in an hour: 16 ♦ *the average speed of released semen:* 28 mph ♦ *the most semen swallowed (verified by stomach pump):* 1.7 pints by Michelle Monaghan, LA, July 1991 ♦ *female gangbang:* a woman called 'Houston' had 620 men in approximately 10 hours (with a few breaks), averaging around 58 seconds per man – the action was recorded on video ♦ *most female orgasms in an hour:* 134 ♦ *male gangbang:* 55 women in one day by porn star Jon Dough – he had five to six ejaculations ♦ *male record over 30 years:* one man had intercourse 52,000 times, averaging 33.3 times a week. (source: clipmarks)

'I didn't kill nobody; I didn't rape no children; I had sex with a woman who wasn't my wife. It was wrong, but I paid for it.'
Boris Becker, admitting to sex in a cupboard at a Nobu restaurant

THE FAN

At the age of 72, Sophia Loren, 'the most beautiful woman in the world', hasn't lost her naughty streak. The Italian sex symbol told *Gazzetta dello Sport* that she would do a striptease if her football team Napoli won promotion and went up to Serie A.

Dennis Rodman

The Chicago Bulls NBA star has been known for cross-dressing, a relationship with Madonna and marriage to Carmen Electra. Not one to be labelled, he has appeared on the cover of *The Advocate* and told *Sports Illustrated* he had only thought about sex with men, but was not gay, adding that mentally he was probably bisexual. Reportedly he used his relaxed sexual persona during the game, catching opponents off guard by asking them for dates.

'I think that making love is the best form of exercise.' Cary Grant

SPORTING BODIES

The *Sports Illustrated Swimsuit Issue* has featured tennis players Stefi Graf, Serena Williams and Anna Kournikova, who has also appeared in *FHM* and *Maxim* and several top sexy and beautiful lists. Olympic competitors volleyball player Gabrielle Reece and high jumper Amy Acuff, plus Olympic golds figure skater Katarina Witt and swimmer Amanda Beard, have all posed for *Playboy*. WWE star Vito LoGrasso has appeared in *Playgirl*, while in 2007 *New Woman* magazine's top 100 sexiest men list included Chelsea football coach José Mourinho and footballers Thierry Henry and David Beckham. Angry football fans protested when Brazilian *Playboy* featured Ana Paula De Oliveira, a controversial referee's assistant, in 13 erotic poses in their July 2007 edition. Head referee Edson Rezende said, 'Being naked in *Playboy* isn't the way forward for officials.' FIFA have withdrawn her accreditation.

'In Holland and Spain and France, where so many of us come from, people aren't interested in the sex lives of their players. We don't hear these stories – even in Italy where the media is right on top of football.' Dennis Bergkamp, talking about the UK press

RECORD BREAKERS

From the prolific and the infamous to great discoveries and achievements, here's where going the distance and size really did matter.

Guinness World Records: The Best Adult World Records (2003)

LARGEST NATURAL BREASTS: Annie Hawkins-Turner, aka Norma Stitz, US size 521 bra, under-breast 43in, around-chest-over-nipple 70in.

OLDEST MALE STRIPPER: Bernie Barker, born 31 July 1940, began stripping in 2000.

MOST EXPENSIVE BRA: Victoria's Secret 'Red Hot Fantasy' bra at $15 million, made with diamonds and rubies.

COSTLIEST EMAIL: £1.3 million to settle a sexual harassment lawsuit filed by four women employees against Chevron Corp.

LONGEST-RUNNING THEATRICAL COMEDY: *No Sex Please: We're British* ran for 16 years and three months in the UK, with 6,761 performances.

MOST GENDER-AWARE ROBOT: Robotic head Doki has visual gender recognition software developed by Intelligent Earth, UK. Doki recognizes 100 per cent of women and 96 per cent of men as well as being able to scientifically rate the attractiveness of women.

The Kinsey Institute and British Library each have about 20,000 books on sex.

♦♦♦

The Vatican Library is said to have about 25,000 volumes on the subject to keep abreast of their favourite topic.

NAKEDWORLDRECORDS.COM

★ The largest penis was recorded by Dr Robert L Dickinson in the early 20th century at 13.5in long and 6.25in circumference.

★ The most valuable nude photos are of a 22-year-old Marilyn Monroe, taken by Tom Kelley. At an auction in 2001, bidding reached $475,000, but the pics remained unsold as the bid didn't meet the reserve price.

★ In 1999, the world's most downloaded naked woman was Danni Ashe, nude model and ex-stripper, with 240 million hits.

★ The first male full frontal nude in *Playboy* was Johnny Crawford in September 1973. With 11 appearances, Pamela Anderson has been on the cover of *Playboy* more than anyone else.

★ In Mexico City in May 2007, approximately 18,000 naked men and women posed for US photographer Spencer Tunick.

World sex records

Louis XV of France's personal royal harem in the Parc aux Cerfs cost about $20m a year. ❋ According to Kinsey, one man had three orgasms a day for 30 years, while another had about 33 a week for 30 years. ❋ In their research, sex experts Masters and Johnson witnessed more than 10,000 male and female orgasms. ❋ The furthest-flung female ejaculation is about 3 metres. ❋ Abu'l Hayjeh is recorded as deflowering 80 virgins in one night. ❋ The world's longest clitoris, featured in W Francis Benedict's *The Sexual Anatomy of Women*, comes in at 12 inches. ❋ Mae West was the oldest sex symbol at an unheard of 40 when she first arrived in Hollywood. ❋ The whale has the biggest vagina in the animal kingdom, at approximately 6 to 8ft long. ❋ The rorqual whale has the largest penis up to 10ft long and 1ft wide. ❋ The average woman burns off between 70 and 120 calories per hour during sex, compared to 77 and 155 for the average man.

EXPRESSIONS

Love and sex can often seem like another language. Understanding each other's desires and denials is often a case of reading the signs and appreciating the gesture.

'If you don't like my peaches, why do you shake my tree?'
Mae West

Handkerchief Code

Popular in the 1970s, this also applies to bandanas and flags. Normally associated with gay men, the system made it easier to recognize each other in bars, parks, the street and clubs. Colour and how the hanky was worn would indicate sexual interests, partners and the possibility of casual sex. Apparently, the code was originally used during the Gold Rush in America, when, due to a lack of women, men had to dance with each other. The bandanas would signify which partner was taking the lead and which was in place of the girl. Today, the hanky's position in the back pocket reveals a preference of 'top' or 'bottom' and the kind of sex sought.

Left: TOP/GIVES   **Right:** BOTTOM/WANTS
RED: anything goes
MUSTARD: food fetish
YELLOW: golden showers
GRAY: bondage
WHITE LACE: Gothic romance
BLACK: Heavy S&M

♦ ALBANIA: *'Sworn virgins' are women who dress like men and live their lives as men.*

♦ BRAZIL: *Homosexuality is signified by an earring in the left ear for men and a left anklet chain for women.*

♦ EGYPT: *The ancient Ankh* ♀ *represents life and the power of the sun, but it is also suggested by many to be sexual – the stem as the male organ holding the circle at the top as the female sex organ, and crossed by children.*

♦ FRANCE: *Napoleon issued monetary fines of 35 francs to men who lifted women's skirts to the knee: raising them to the thigh cost 70 francs .*

♦ GERMANY: *Apparently, there are 30 words for kissing and a word for the ones that haven't been invented yet –* Nachkuss.

♦ ITALY: *In 15th-century Venice, prostitutes had to display their breasts when they were visible from open windows, so they could not be confused with the general female public.*

♦ JAVA: *In some areas, couples have* sex *in fields to encourage crops to grow.*

♦ NEW GUINEA: *The reason some elderly men are missing fingers is because the custom was to give a girlfriend a lucky digit to wear around her neck before a fight. Meanwhile, on the island of Trobriand, biting off a woman's eyelashes is a passionate activity.*

♦ USA: *In California in the 1940s, some drag queens pinned signs to their dresses saying, 'I'm a boy,' to avoid the law against serving alcohol to a homosexual or a man wearing women's clothing. Technically, they were dressed as a man.*

♦ WALES: *It is said that in the 18th century men gave carved wooden spoons to show their love for a woman, which she would wear around her neck or hang in a window to show she felt the same.*

♦ ZAMBIA: *When greeting women, eye contact is avoided by men to prevent the possible miscommunication of desire. By the same token, women are not expected to shake hands.*

'Love is just a system for getting someone to call you darling after sex.' Julian Barnes, *Talking It Over*, 1991

Star sex

☆ ARIES Intense, open-minded, dominant, enjoys the chase

☆ TAURUS Appealing, deep, insatiable, strong, cosy, loyal

☆ GEMINI Adventurous, enjoys variety, desires stimulation, tolerant

☆ CANCER Profound, intuitive, steamy, caring, loves making love

☆ LEO Wild, dynamic, protective, loves attention and compliments

☆ VIRGO Sensitive, considerate, steady, devoted in a meeting of minds

☆ LIBRA Energetic, considerate, sensual, loves praise and luxury

☆ SCORPIO Natural libido, voracious, dominant, hypnotizing

☆ SAGITTARIUS Passionate, lusty, lively, impulsive, fun, honest

☆ CAPRICORN Shy, underlying passion, loves stimulation, faithful

☆ AQUARIUS Heart and mind connection, rampant, creative, loyal

☆ PISCES Emotional, sensual, playful, appetite for fantasies

Sex Symbols

- The male gender sign is represented by the shield of the god Mars, with an arrow pointing northeast
- The female gender sign is represented by a circle and cross symbol said to be the hand mirror and comb of the goddess Venus

'No type of attitude is more fundamental and more indicative of the trend of Personality than are attitudes to sexual matters.'
Gordon Rattray Taylor, *Sex In History*, 1954

'Being a sex symbol was rather like being a convict.'   Raquel Welch

---

NAIL FILE

King Victor Emmanuel of Italy had his own style of etiquette when it came to sending his mistresses personal gifts. Each year, he would grow his big toenail, have it polished and bejewelled and then have it sent to the latest lady in his life.

TATTOOS

Research has found that 34 per cent of Americans with tattoos feel sexier, with 42 per cent being women as opposed to 25 per cent of men, while 26 per cent revealed that their body art made them feel more attractive. However, of those without, 42 per cent felt people with tattoos were less attractive and 36 per cent said they were not as sexy. Popular designs include the Venus symbol, and many have meanings behind them, such as the devil which implies a desire for sex. The rose means fertility, a wolf fidelity and a unicorn represents chastity.

'Once they call you a Latin Lover, you're in real trouble. Women expect an Oscar performance in bed.' Marcello Mastroianni

SEX GODS AND GODDESSES

❤AEVAL Celtic goddess of sex and small size. When dissatisfied wives took their husbands to court, she judged whether the men were doing enough to please them.

❤AISHA QANDISHA Moroccan goddess of sexual activity, who appeared as a beauty or a hag and was best obeyed when it came to her rampant demands.

❤EROS (Roman: Cupid) Greek god of erotic love also known for his impish ways, this winged son of Aphrodite and Ares launched two types of arrows: one kind created passion, the other caused indifference. Often blindfolded, he illustrated the fact that love is blind.

❤FREYA Viking goddess of sensuality and fertility, said to be the most beautiful. One of her best-known features is the Necklace of the Brisings, obtained from four dwarves who demanded she sleep with each of them in return for the coveted jewellery.

❤HERMAPHRODITUS Greek son of Hermes and Aphrodite who was fused with a nymph, making him partly male, partly female.

❤KAMA Indian god of love and desire, who was accompanied by a honeybee. His arrows injected a sensual selection of satisfaction, prowess and libido.

❤LEMPO Finnish lord of all evil and demons, and shockingly, also the Finnish god of love.

❤LOFN Viking goddess who revelled in forbidden love and illicit unions.

❤P'AN CHIN-LIEN Chinese goddess of prostitutes.

❤SJOFN Norse goddess who put the passion back into failing marriages.

❤TLAZOLTEOTL Aztec goddess of love, licentiousness and sex, also the 'eater of filth'. Men confessed their sins, which she consumed before they met their death.

❤YARILO Slavic god represented on a white horse, embracing spring, fertility and virility.

APHRODITE (ROMAN: VENUS)

The ancient Greek goddess of erotic love and beauty, her name is the root of 'aphrodisiac'. Her powers could requite longing, as shown in the tale of the sculptor Pygmalion who had never found a woman worth loving. Inspired by Aphrodite, he created and fell in love with an ivory statue, which he married when the goddess brought her to life. Even Aphrodite's own relationships were fraught. Zeus, who feared her sexual allure and beauty would cause wars among men, forced her to marry grim smith Hephaestus, who unwittingly gave her a magic girdle making her even more irresistible, thereby encouraging numerous affairs. One such conquest, the perfect male mortal Adonis, was murdered by jealous lover Ares, god of war and son of Zeus, whose own affair with Aphrodite was discovered by her husband and punished with public ridicule. Zeus's fears proved to be well founded when Aphrodite was the direct cause of the Trojan War. In a contest for the title of fairest goddess, Zeus appointed Paris as judge. Though he declined all other bribes, he could not resist the temptation of Aphrodite's offer of the most beautiful mortal in the world – Helen.

Mighty Aphrodite

In the 1996 Woody Allen comedy, with ideas linked to Oedipus and Pygmalion, Mira Sorvino won Best Supporting Actress Oscar for her role as the ditsy porn star birthmother of an adopted boy looking for his roots.

Oedipus Complex

Unaware of his adoptive status, Oedipus became King of Thebes by killing his natural father and marrying his natural mother. Freud used this myth to construct his theory that a male child's unconscious longing for his father's death was necessary to fulfil his unconscious craving to be the sole recipient of his mother's love.

APHRODISIACS

'Fetch me that flower, the herb I show'd thee once;
The juice of it on sleeping eyelids laid
Will make man or woman madly dote
Upon the next live creature that it sees.'
Oberon, *A Midsummer Night's Dream*

POTENT OR PLACEBO EFFECT?

Throughout history, aphrodisiacs, with their natural and physical properties pertaining to sex, have been used as sexual enhancers, inadequacy remedies and to encourage fertility. The promotion and sale of these love-makers, including scents, foods and drugs, is a multibillion-dollar industry, though modern science says there is little evidence to support most claims of libido-boosting properties. Despite this, lovers everywhere have always been attracted to these arousal aids, which often prove successful with the help of the most powerful aphrodisiac there is – the mind.

'There is no aphrodisiac like innocence.'
Jean Baudrillard, French philosopher

Spanish Fly

Actually made from a blister beetle, this can cause burning, vomiting and kidney failure among other unpleasant side-effects, but it has still been desired throughout history since it is supposed to produce record amounts of sexual activity. Registered as a Class One poison and illegal in most countries, it is permissible for animal husbandry in the US, while the German *Spanische Fliege* is only obtainable in a safe homeopathic dosage.

'There is no scientific proof that any over-the-counter aphrodisiacs work to treat sexual dysfunction.' US Food and Drug Administration

Food of love

Many foods gain their aphrodisiacal reputations from form and texture as well as nutritionally sexual qualities. A sample from the menu:

Herbs Popular varieties include Kava Kava, which relaxes the spine but not the mind, and Damiana, often used in tea to brew up passion.

Avocado Hangs in pairs from the *ahuacatl* (testicle tree) and was named thus by the Aztecs due to the curvy, fleshy fruit's resemblance to those male attributes.

Tiger's penis Some Asian cultures believe it increases male virility, while also encouraging the penis to become larger.

Potatoes Thought to be the answer to everything and called 'apples of love' in Shakespearean times.

Asparagus Top tip: 'Consume over three consecutive days for the most powerful effect,' says the Vegetarian Society.

Onions Ancient Egyptian priests were forbidden to eat these tearjerkers in case they couldn't control their sexual urges, forcing them to break their oath of celibacy.

Rat poison In the 19th century, an extremely minute portion was taken to cause a pleasurable irritation to the sexual organs.

Human genitals, menstrual blood and semen Believed to step up the libido in ancient China, which led to cannibalism.

Raw natural, uncooked food, ginseng tea, eaten al fresco and with fingers is the modern way.

'A number of rare or newly experienced foods have been claimed to be aphrodisiacs. At one time this quality was even ascribed to the tomato. Reflect on that when you are next preparing the family salad.' Jane Grigson, cookery writer

CHOCOLATE

One of the most popular aphrodisiacs, originally from South America, where the Aztec and Mayan cultures worshipped its magically passionate effects. Later discovered by the Spanish, it was soon introduced to the rest of the world. Phenylethylamine and serotonin, found in chocolate, encourage a feeling of pleasure when released into the body, accounting for the substance's widespread reputation.

ABC of 'sexy' ingredients

Antlers, **B**ull's testicles, **C**abbage, **D**onuts, turtle **E**ggs, **F**rog's legs, **G**arlic, rhino **H**orn, **I**ce cream, **J**ava coffee, **K**umquat, **L**obster, **M**ango, **N**ail clippings, **O**kra, seal's **P**enis, **Q**uince, **R**ice, **S**hark fin, **T**equila, **U**nagi, **V**anilla, **W**ine, **X**anat, **Y**east, **Z**ucchini.

Oysters

Likened to female sex organs, Casanova had a penchant for fifty servings of this delicacy for breakfast. If this was not proof enough of their effects on the sex drive, in 2005 American and Italian researchers discovered that oysters are rich in rare amino acids, not found naturally elsewhere, which help increase sex hormones.

'I placed the shell on the edge of her lips and after a good deal of laughing, she sucked in the oyster, which she held between her lips. I instantly recovered it by placing my lips on hers.' Casanova

Liquorice root, the Great Harmonizer, has long been used as an aphrodisiac, from ancient China to the *Kama Sutra*.

♦♦♦

Liquorice root has also been reported as having exactly the opposite effect by suppressing the libido.

Viagra

Originally seen as a treatment for angina, Pfizer first patented Viagra in 1996 as a cure for impotence. Peter Dunn and Albert Wood, reported in the press as the inventors, are named on the manufacturing patent. The first pill of its kind in the USA, it was approved by the FDA and went on sale in 1998. Within two weeks, doctors were writing 40,000 prescriptions a day. It has since been prescribed to more than 23 million men.

Following the approval of Viagra by the UK health authorities, a shipment arrived at Heathrow airport but was hijacked on the way to the pharmacy warehouse. Scotland Yard has asked the public to look out for a gang of hardened criminals.

ANAPHRODISIACS

Suppressors of the sex drive ♦ Anti-androgen drugs are prescribed to recurring sex offenders and have side-effects, including hair loss, headaches and breast development ♦ Cigarettes and alcohol taken in excess actively decrease sexual prowess.

'I told her that I was a flop with chicks
I've been this way since 1956
She looked at my palm and she made a magic sign
She said, "What you need is Love Potion Number Nine."'
The Clovers, 'Love Potion Number 9', 1959

SEX AND POWER

*'If I don't have a woman every three days or so
I get a terrible headache.'* John F Kennedy

ADOLF HITLER (1889–1945) The sexuality of the architect of Nazism remains somewhat obscure, while rumours have hinted at deviancy or fetishism of some kind. He is thought to have had a relationship with his niece, Geli Raubal, and one witness claims they indulged in urolagia ('golden showers') together. German women often became hysterical in the presence of the Führer. This much-questioned attraction is explained by many psychologists who believe some women are simply attracted to power. All three women with whom Hitler is thought to have been intimate – Raubal, Eva Braun and a fiancée from the 1920s – attempted suicide.
MARQUIS DE SADE (1740–1814) The source of the term 'sadism', meaning enjoyment of cruelty, was a French aristocrat and writer of extreme pornography who spent a total of 32 years incarcerated in either prisons or asylums. He pursued a career of sexual violence towards prostitutes and household servants of both sexes, helped at times by his wife. He was frequently accused of attempting to sodomize fellow prison inmates. Fat and 50, he embarked on one last affair with a 13-year-old girl employed at the asylum at Charenton where he was to die in 1814.

CHARLES MANSON (1934–) Career criminal Manson cashed in on the 1960s free love ethos to form The Family, a cult that comprised mainly young

*'I respect and admire the fairer sex/
And I honour them every bit as much as the next misogynist.'*
Jake Thackeray, 'On One Issue at Least'

women. Using a weird blend of Scientology and misinterpretations of Beatles lyrics, he persuaded a group of his followers to carry out a series of ritualistic-looking murders, including the killing of film star Sharon Tate.

RASPUTIN (1872–1916) The charismatic spiritualist with a reputation for sexual licentiousness, which included the accusation that he raped a nun, so beguiled the Emperor and especially the Empress of Russia when he apparently cured their haemophiliac son that he became the Empress's personal confidant and adviser. He started a cult mixing Christianity with sex and was soon having it off with a selection of aristocratic women who hoped for political favours in return.

↘ *Rasputin's 30 cm penis is preserved in the St Petersburg sex museum. Founder Igor Knyazkin commented, 'We can stop envying America where Napoleon Bonaparte's penis is now kept. Napoleon's penis is but a small "pod". It can stand no comparison to our own organ of 30 centimetres.'*

Unbelievable

Jimmy Swaggart, US televangelist and cousin of Jerry Lee Lewis, had a weakness for prostitutes which was his undoing in 1988 when photographs of him were taken with whores. His fall was all the harder given that he had just named and shamed rival televangelist Marvin Gorman for the same sins.

'Man has his will, but woman has her way.'
Oliver Wendell Holmes, *The Autocrat of the Breakfast Table*, 1858

✳

'I don't see so much of Alfred since he got so interested in sex.'
Mrs Alfred Kinsey

CROWNING GLORIES

'I don't think a prostitute is more moral than a wife, but they are doing the same thing.' Prince Philip, Duke of Edinburgh

MISTRESSES AND KINGS

King Charles II, the Merry Monarch, had at least 13 mistresses, of whom the most famous was Nell Gwyn (see p.167). George II had two German mistresses known by their nicknames: the tall, thin one was 'The Maypole', while the short, fat one was 'the Elephant and Castle'. The King spent many happy evenings with the latter 'indulging their shared passion for cutting out paper pictures'. Louis XIV, the Sun King, had so many mistresses he hardly knew what to do: whenever he wanted to travel with his actual mistress, he had to take his wife as well as his official mistress along with him for propriety's sake. Edward VII, Queen Victoria's successor, was a notorious playboy and his list of mistresses included actresses Lillie Langtry and Sarah Bernhardt, Alice Keppel (Camilla Parker-Bowles's great-grandmother) and Jennie Jerome (Winston Churchill's mother). As a young prince George IV fell for actress Mary Robinson, aka Perdita, and promised her a large sum of money when he came of age. When their affair ended he did not stump up, so she threatened to reveal his love letters to George III. He paid. His true love was widow Mrs Maria Fitzherbert who he was not permitted to marry as she was a Catholic. But he married her anyway. The marriage was ruled invalid and he was forced by his father to marry Caroline of Brunswick, but she turned his stomach rather than his head. He was still focused on Mrs Fitzherbert, with whom he would later resume his relationship.

'A man needs the sexual conquest to prove that he can still do it, that he can still get it up. It's like having a duel with himself. He has to prove it all the time. We don't have to prove it.'
Princess Elizabeth of Yugoslavia

QUEENS

Several kings of England were rumoured to be gay and some most certainly were. James I had a succession of male lovers, including the Earl of Somerset and George Villiers whom he referred to as his 'sweet child and wife'. Extraordinarily handsome, Villiers rose from the humble post of royal cupbearer to Gentleman of the Bedchamber and finally to Earl of Buckingham. Edward II had a 'lifelong very good friend' in Piers Gaveston, who was decapitated by jealous nobles in 1312. Edward met a terrible end in 1327 when he was tortured to death by his wife Isabella and her lover Roger Mortimer, harsh treatment which included a red-hot poker up the backside. Other homosexual monarchs include Richard the Lionheart and Queen Anne who maintained a lifelong passion for Sarah Jennings, despite the fact that both were married.

Catherine the Great

The Russian empress, who ruled as a so-called enlightened despot in the late 18th century, was infamous for the number of lovers she had. She married Grand Duke Peter in 1745, but he was simple-minded and preferred playing with his toy soldiers and dogs to playing with her. A problem with his foreskin also made sex impossible until he was circumcised. In the meantime, his wife developed a taste for young military men and had her bedroom curtained off, so she could receive lovers in private but only after they had been vetted by the court physician. This also turned out to be a convenient way of supplying the Grand Duke's heirs. One of her most passionate affairs was with Prince Grigory Potemkin, who, once his purpose was served, helped her find suitable subsequent lovers. The last of her paramours, who was with her until her death at the age of 67, was a prince 40 years her junior. Some people say Catherine had 300 lovers, but a figure in the low teens might be nearer the mark.

SEX IN HIGH PLACES

*'You men are unaccountable things: mad till you have your
mistresses, and then stark mad till you are rid of 'em again.'*
Sir John Vanbrugh, *The Provok'd Wife,* 1697

MADAME DE POMPADOUR

An intelligent and beautiful woman, she cleverly landed herself the
role of mistress of Louis XV of France, following the death of her
predecessor the Duchess of Châteauroux. The sexual aspects of her
position lasted about five years until around 1750, after which she

remained in the king's favour as his confidante and began
choosing his new mistresses for him. It is rumoured that
the *coupe de Champagne* glass was modelled on her
breast, but this has also been said of Marie Antoinette
and Joséphine de Beauharnais, first wife of Napoleon.

The Dirty Duchess

Margaret Whigham (1912–1993) had a taste for millionaires and
playboys, but following a near fatal fall down an elevator shaft during her
first marriage, the then Mrs Sweeny's injuries induced raving
nymphomania. Many relationships later, the vain socialite married the
11th Duke of Argyll earning her a title. Scandal arrived with a series of
Polaroids showing the Duchess wearing only a pearl necklace and
pleasuring an unidentified naked man; her good name was further
tarnished when her husband introduced a list of 88 men, with whom he
suspected she had had sexual encounters, to the divorce court. In the
hunt to uncover the 'headless man' of the images, suspects included
Douglas Fairbanks Jr and former Minister of Defence Duncan Sandys,
adding a bit of star quality to an already sensational case.

Amour courtois

The idea of courtly love developed in France at the time of the First Crusade in the late 11th century and it still informs our sense of what constitutes true love. This poetic notion was as idealistic as it was romantic and it came to embrace its own set of commandments.

FROM *THE ART OF COURTLY LOVE* BY ANDREAS CAPELLANUS (C. 1186)

1 *Thou shalt avoid avarice like the deadly pestilence and shalt embrace its opposite.*

2 *Thou shalt keep thyself chaste for the sake of her whom thou lovest.*

3 *Thou shalt not knowingly strive to break up a correct love affair that someone else is engaged in.*

4 *Thou shalt not choose for thy love anyone whom a natural sense of shame forbids thee to marry.*

5 *Be mindful completely to avoid falsehood.*

6 *Thou shalt not have many who know of thy love affair.*

7 *Being obedient in all things to the commands of ladies, thou shalt ever strive to ally thyself to the service of Love.*

8 *In giving and receiving love's solaces let modesty be ever present.*

9 *Thou shalt speak no evil.*

10 *Thou shalt not be a revealer of love affairs.*

11 *Thou shalt be in all things polite and courteous.*

12 *In practising the solaces of love thou shalt not exceed the desires of thy lover.*

HOW THE OTHER HALF LOVED

➤ In France in the 13th century young women were kept in *gynaecea* – or *chambres de dames* – where they were available 24/7 exclusively for the lord's pleasure. Count Baudouin, for example, had access to his servant girls' quarters along with the bedroom of practically every female in his castle. When he died, 33 of his officially recognized children turned up for the burial and 23 of them were bastards.

➤ When Lord Aboyne and Lord Moray left London's Wig Club in 1775, they made off with the object that gave the club its name, a wig woven out of the pubic hair of Charles II's mistresses. Members brought along a lock of their own mistresses' hidden tresses to be added in.

➤ Inspired by the experiments of Benjamin Franklin, infamous quack Dr James Graham invented a 'medico-magnetico-musico-electrical bed', built on 28 glass pillars with a mattress of stallion hair and a magnificent mirrored dome. Surrounded by fluxing magnetic lodestones, the Celestial Bed was designed 'to produce strong, beautiful, brilliant, nay double-distilled children' and wealthy 18th-century couples allegedly paid £50 to rekindle their passion upon it. The beautiful 16-year-old Emma Lyon – later Lady Hamilton – further enhanced the bed's charms by dancing round it stark naked. Graham's clients included the Prince of Wales.

➤ In Venice in the late Middle Ages, 'sodomy' was particularly common among the clergy and, where this involved homosexuality, the punishment could be castration or even hanging. At this time, coitus interruptus was still classed as 'sodomy', historically an elastic term for anything the authorities wanted to suppress. Masturbation was acceptable until the Plague arrived and the population rapidly dwindled. The 'wasting of seed' suddenly became a criminal offence.

➤ Jean-Jacques Rousseau admitted in his *Confessions* he masturbated while remembering childhood beatings from his foster mother.

➤ 1911 was the original Summer of Love in England. When temperatures hit 100°F, the Edwardian upper classes adopted flimsy clothes and morals to match. Lady Cunard cuckolded her husband with conductor Thomas Beecham, Lord Curzon embarked on an affair with writer Elinor Glyn and Lord Charles Beresford leapt lustily on to the bed of his girlfriend shouting 'Cock-a-doodle-do', only to discover he'd jumped upon a dozing Bishop of Chester.

FOOLING THE PUBLIC

Lavender marriages are marriages of convenience where one or more partner is homosexual. Composer Jean-Baptiste Lully (1632–87), Louis XIV's favourite, wed Madeleine Lambert and had ten children by her which was above and beyond the call of duty for a man who merely wanted to conceal the love he had for his page Brunet. Lully died of gangrene after stabbing his toe with a cane he was using to keep time. ❋ Vasily II, father of Ivan the Terrible, could only have sex with his wife when there was a naked guardsman in bed with them. ❋ Frederick the Great married Elisabeth Christine of Brunswick-Bevern in 1733, but when his father died in 1740 he banned her from visiting his court. In later years, Frederick retired to a palace called Sans Soucis where cultural interchanges were lively but women were never part of them.

Famous lavender marriages: André Gide and Madeleine Rondeaux; Prince de Polignac and Henrietta Singer; Charles Laughton and Elsa Lanchester; Vita Sackville-West and Harold Nicolson; Rock Hudson and Phyllis Gates

LAYDEEZ AND GENTLEMEN

In 1870 Ernest Boulton and Frederick William Park were arrested at the Strand Theatre, London, dressed in full evening frocks and travelling under the names of Lady Stella Clinton and Miss Fanny Park. The police had been watching them for some time. Charged with conspiracy to commit buggery – being a transvestite was just a misdemeanour – both appeared in the dock arrayed magnificently in full drag: Boulton in a fetching wig and 'a cherry-coloured silk evening dress' and Park in green satin 'with his flaxen hair in curls'. Since sodomy could not be proved, they were later acquitted to great rejoicing in the public gallery.

IT'S ONLY ROCK'N'ROLL...

But musicians seem to like sex as much as their music. And some of their fans have been pretty keen too.

✦ Ludwig van Beethoven may have pined after his 'Immortal Beloved' – the mysterious woman to whom he poured out his heart – but his liaisons weren't always as romantic. Beethoven scholars have revealed that he frequently visited prostitutes, while there's even conjecture in academic circles that his famous deafness was caused by syphilis.

✦ After the Cold War thawed out, historians confirmed what had long been suppressed by the authorities – Tchaikovsky was gay. He chose to marry, to keep up appearances and for his own sanity, but couldn't hide his feelings for nephew Vladimir. Shortly before he died, Tchaikovsky dedicated his Sixth Symphony to the boy he called 'Bob', telling him in a letter that it contained 'a programme which shall remain a mystery for every one'.

✦ Acclaimed pianist and composer Percy Grainger (1882–1961) never bothered to hide his sexual proclivities, writing to a correspondent, 'by 16, I was already sex-crazy'. An outspoken fan of sado-masochism, he admitted that whipping and being whipped were just as important as creating and playing his music. 'To empty oneself out, in art or sex, is the acme of all life,' he wrote. 'Constipation, of all kinds, is the root of all downheartedness.'

✦ Composers were once considered the rock stars of their day, and just like today's musical heroes, you couldn't tie many of them down to just one relationship. Antonio Vivaldi wasn't happy just to set up home with a 15-year-old soprano – he also had a long-standing love affair with her sister Paolina. Despite censure from the Pope and others, the happy threesome travelled together to Vivaldi's musical engagements.

✦ And just like today's rock stars classical composers were never short of groupies. Four major composers, Franz Peter Schubert, Robert Schumann, Hugo Wolf and Frederick Delius – all died through the primary or secondary effects of syphilis.

✦ Self-confessed 'recovering groupie' Cynthia Plaster Caster began taking life-size plaster replicas of famous rockers' penises back in 1968. Having re-created the members of some of the world's greatest rock bands, from psychedelic rocker Jimi Hendrix to political punk Jello Biafra of the Dead Kennedys, she diversified into the casting of female artists' breasts in 2000, including Peaches and Karen O.

✦ As author of the tell-all Led Zeppelin biography, *Hammer of the Gods*, Stephen Davis is responsible for spreading one of the greatest backstage rock'n'roll stories of all time. The 'red snapper' incident, as it's known, had the band pleasure a red-headed young groupie with various parts of a fish. The band members don't deny it happened, but claim the girl in question wasn't hurt or abused in any way.

✦ Rockbitch caused controversy by interspersing their sets with nudity, pagan ritual and simulated lesbian sex. The most infamous part of their show was the 'Golden Condom' contest. The condom in question was thrown into the audience and the man or woman who caught it was supposedly taken backstage to get intimate with the band.

✦ Ex-Jethro Tull keyboardist, David Palmer has had a sex change and is known as Dee. A former Royal Horse Guard, he now sings mezzo-soprano and plays piano under the name of 'Granny D'.

'I think I mentioned to Bob [Geldof] I could make love for eight hours. What I didn't say was that this included four hours of begging and then dinner and a movie.' Sting on tantric sex

SEX CLUBS

'It's been so long since I made love,
I can't even remember who gets tied up.'
Joan Rivers

THE EVE CLUB

In the 1960s, the Eve club in Soho was one of the few places in town where you could see an erotic floor show. This featured 'the most beautiful showgirls in London', although full nudity was forbidden and *les girls'* movements on stage were restricted in line with the morality of the time. John Profumo had his stag night there, the Bishop of Southwell's wife was a former hostess and stars like Frank Sinatra and Errol Flynn used to drop by to 'relax', along with government ministers, peers of the realm, diplomats, MI5 operatives and other spies. Sex might have been available, but it was never on the club's official menu as the 1962 brochure made clear in describing a star turn: 'Her attractions are stunning, her talent is extraordinary and her telephone number, sir, is none of your business.' By the 1990s, the Eve Club was old hat and closed down. A revived Eve Club opened round the corner in 2003, a pale shadow of its former self.

'Chastity – the most unnatural of all the sexual perversions.' Aldous Huxley

Ping Pong Shows

These ball-without-the-bat shows are common in Thai sex tourism entertainment, where women demonstrate the power of the pelvic muscle to expel objects from the vagina. Talents include writing with pens, shooting fruit and smoking cigarettes. Audience participation in the act is often demanded which can involve holding a target to test accuracy.

TALKING JAPANESE

The sexual imagination of the Japanese knows few boundaries, starting with clubs populated by pretend nurses, fake air hostesses and phoney secretaries. Other specialities include: rotating sushi-style breast-fondling clubs; special 'Marilyn features' – you watch as she stands over a hot air-vent; naked karaoke; soapgirls, notably 'handpicked brides' who bathe customers; anime clubs (sex with manga characters); 'police investigation' clubs where guests fight over who gets to wear the 'cuffs; and fake train carriages where up to 14 customers at a time get to grope underdressed women in steamy rush-hour conditions.

Amora

This deep and meaningful sex theme park calling itself a 'love and relationships academy' opened in London's Piccadilly in April 2007. Interactive 'rides' include an Orgasm Tunnel, Spankometer, stripping class and tactile erogenous zones. These hands-on seductions intend to provide an educational sexual experience that visitors can take away inspiring them to become better lovers.

NOW AND THEN

Amsterdam's red light district, famous as a sexual destination since the 14th century, is also home to the Venus Temple sex museum. Open since 1985, a satyr with an erection welcomes visitors to an exhibition of artefacts, including an ancient stone phallus and an iron chastity belt. In New York, the Fifth Avenue Sex Museum was founded in 2002 with an award-winning opening exhibition 'NYCSEX: How New York Changed Sex in America'. As well as collections from clothing to photography, it also holds events, such as discussions about sex on the Internet and even 'how to' classes, which have included blow jobs.

SCANDALS

'You find out who your real friends are when you're involved in a scandal.' Liz Taylor

The Profumo Affair

MP John Profumo's political career was ruined when news broke in 1963 that he had shared a mistress (albeit unknowingly) with an attaché at the Soviet embassy. The woman in the middle was topless showgirl Christine Keeler who was immortalized in Lewis Morley's photograph of her posing nude astride a chair, one of the iconic images of the 1960s.

GETTING AWAY WITH IT

★DAVID MELLOR *Another British Conservative MP caused a sensation when his sexual exploits with actress Antonia de Sancha in 1992 hit the papers – after she sold them the story. Mellor's career survived the fallout from the affair, but not the later uproar over free holidays.*

★HUGH GRANT *Making an unforgettable Hollywood appearance, the poster boy for foppish English charm suffered few personal or professional setbacks in 1995 upon being caught by the vice squad receiving oral sex from sex worker Divine Brown on Sunset Boulevard.*

★BILL CLINTON *The 42nd president of the USA likewise endured little lasting damage following revelations that he had had sexual relations with intern Monica Lewinsky in 1998. She had confided her feelings to a colleague, who recorded phone conversations leading to Clinton's impeachment for perjury, but he was later acquitted. Apparently, he didn't realize oral sex was included in the definition of 'sexual relations'.*

'Clinton lied. A man might forget where he parks or where he lives, but he never forgets oral sex, no matter how bad it is.' Barbara Bush

'I regret to say that we of the FBI are powerless to act in cases of oral-genital intimacy, unless it has in some way obstructed interstate commerce.' J Edgar Hoover

THE ONE THAT DIDN'T GET AWAY

JEFFREY ARCHER The novelist and MP came unstuck on perjury charges following newspaper allegations of his liaison with prostitute Monica Coghlan. He served two years in prison and had his membership of the Marylebone Cricket Club suspended for seven years.

PARIS HILTON

The hotel heiress declared she was quitting one-night stands on *Live with Regis and Kelly* in June 2006. Six months later, ParisExposed.com revealed the contents of her locker, including a video allegedly including footage in a bubble bath. Most memorable is her 2003 starring role in *One Night in Paris* with ex Rick Salomon. The sex video shot in a hotel room in 'night vision' was leaked, but later she allowed its release on DVD, winning *Adult Video News* awards for its efforts.

Sex tapes

♦ Figure skater Tonya Harding and husband Jeff Gillooly's performance became so widely available that the couple decided to legally release *Wedding Night* themselves.

♦ A stolen tape of sportscaster and blaxpoitation actress Jayne Kennedy and former husband Leon Isaac Kennedy showed them performing explicit acts such as fisting.

♦ Colin Farrell's 13-minute sex tape with ex and Playmate Nicole Narain was granted a court order to prevent its distribution, but copies still appeared on the internet.

MATTERS OF THE HEART

People do the craziest things for love, but sometimes all it takes is a bit of romance to achieve the heart's desire.

'Birds do it, bees do it,
Even educated fleas do it.
Let's do it, Let's fall in love'
Cole Porter, 'Let's Do It', 1928

FLOWER POWER

Flowers have been used to send coded love messages since ancient times, but the art known as floriography reached its peak during the Victorian era. Each type and colour of flower had its meaning, as did the way in which flowers were presented. Giving with the left hand indicated 'no', and from the right 'yes'. Red roses meant love and desire, yellow roses could indicate infidelity or jealousy, while peach roses were a request to get together with someone. Forget-Me-Nots showed true love and tulips were for the perfect lover. On that subject, if things are a little withered in the bedroom department a vase of watered roses by the bedside can help the libido bloom. The scent comes from phenylethylamine containing amino acids that slow down the breakdown of beta-endorphins – happy hormones encouraging sexual euphoria.

Soft spot for romance

Research by Professor Richard Harris of Kansas State University showed that men enjoy so-called 'chick flicks' too. When he separated a group of men and a group of women and asked them to rate romantic movies, the study revealed that both sexes gave the same ratings. While the women believed men only watched for the sex scenes, many of the men actually preferred the more romantic parts, and when the men said they thought the women loved the romance, they were right.

Love letter acronyms

SWALK sealed with a loving kiss ♥ BOLTOP better on lips than on paper ♥ BURMA be undressed ready my angel ♥ ITALY I trust and love you ♥ NORWICH (k)nickers off ready when I come home ♥ SIAM sexual intercourse at midnight

---

LOVESICK

For many in love the symptoms are bearable, as sickening for devoted bliss can be its own remedy. But, according to recent reports, the consequences of stress from emotional extremes – lack of concentration, no appetite and no sleep – suggest being in love can be too intense to handle, while those whose love is unrequited can also find it hard to cope. Some psychologists believe it is even possible to die of a broken heart as a result of depression and losing the will to carry on.

Love Letters

When a guy from Canada met a girl from Belgium on holiday in Cuba, he fell hard, but unfortunately failed to recover sufficiently to get her number. Believing love can find a way, he wrote to 3,700 Sabines in Belgium and his story spread on the airwaves where a friend of the real Sabine heard his plea and passed on his amorous appeal.

COST OF LOVE

A 2007 poll by MoneyExpert found that the average Brit pays out about £744 a year on their nearest and dearest, with men spending more than women. While diamonds remain a girl's best friend, other top romantic gifts included Koi carp and tattoos.

CONTEMPORARY SEX

*'I'm too shy to express my sexual needs except
over the phone to people I don't know.'* Garry Shandling

Playing the percentages

15 per cent of all adults in the US are having half of all the sex; 25 per cent of wives and 44 per cent of husbands have had extra-marital sex

ACCEPTABLE AFFAIRS?

A survey of online chat rooms highlighted their popularity among people who were married or in serious relationships. Able to discuss fantasies anonymously without actually cheating on a partner, many felt it was harmless fun. However, a spouse may not be so easily convinced, as one blissfully-in-love-yet-unaware wife in America found out. She discovered her partner had been a member of a number of dating and sex sites for several years, posing under various guises and orientations, having cyber sex with men and women, listing weird cravings and, although he did sometimes admit he was married, he also implied that his wife was just a blot on his landscape.

Female retail fantasy

In 2005, Brutal Fruit's 'Fantasy Survey' found 45 per cent of South African women would rather shop, shop, shop than have sex, which didn't even come in second. 'Shoes' even beat sexual fantasies on a tropical island with a partner or a hunk. When it came to love, ironically, 75 per cent of the women wished their partners were more romantic.

MALE REALITY CHECK

A 2005 survey by lifestyle site Askmen.com revealed that 70 per cent strongly believed in marriage, 65 per cent would not cheat even if they could get away with it, only 18 per cent visited a strip club at least once a month and 60 per cent wanted greater variety or simply more sex.

'In my day, I would only have sex with a man if I found him extremely attractive. These days, girls seem to choose them in much the same way as they might choose to suck on a boiled sweet.'
Mary Wesley, British novelist

TOO TIRED

Recent studies reveal that stressed-out Singaporeans have no energy left to enjoy sex. Professor Victor Goh found that Singaporeans only indulged six times a month, while in other countries three times a week was the norm. Research showed that lack of time was responsible. However, only about 40 per cent of the men and 20 per cent of the women below the age of 40 actually expressed a desire for more.

Sleeping Partners

The average number of lifetime sexual partners according to the Durex 2005 global sex survey is:
AMERICA 10.7 ❖ UK 9.8 ❖ AUSTRALIA 13.3 ❖ GERMANY 5.8 ❖ INDIA has the lowest figure with 3 ❖ TURKEY tops the list with 14.5

Symmetry in a woman's features is not related to fidelity.
♦♦♦
The more symmetrical a man's features, the earlier he loses his virginity and the more likely he is to be unfaithful.

Dressing to kill

SEXY LITTLE NUMBERS

Dressing to impress can play a big part in a seduction ritual, with fashions and uniforms often providing sexual confidence and compelling entertainment before the eventual strip.

Dress like an Egyptian

Ancient Egyptian women with polished shaved heads were considered attractive and feminine at a time when cleanliness was of paramount importance. Carrying a cone of scented grease on the head was popular with Egyptian women in 1400BC. The oils dripped on to the skin and clothing, making them shiny and fragrant. When Cleopatra met Mark Antony she was well prepared to get her man, dressed as Venus and accompanied by fan-flapping boys in Cupid costumes. They had sex for days.

'According to a new survey, women say they feel more comfortable undressing in front of men than they do undressing in front of other women. They say that women are too judgmental, whereas, of course, men are just grateful.' Robert de Niro

MERKINS

With a name that sounds like something from the Middle Ages, it's no surprise the pubic wig was invented in 1450 as a substitute cover after a spell of lice infestation and was used later to hide the effects of syphilis and genital warts among prostitutes. Now, they're surprisingly popular. Called 'Night Flowers' in Japan, they are used to make the physically immature look more like fully developed women.

'I'm just looking for that moment to drop my Jedi knickers and pull out my real light saber.' Ewan McGregor after his foray in *Star Wars*

T-shirt slogans

'Making Love – That's What My Girlfriend Does When
I'm Fucking Her'❖'Don't Be Sexist, Broads Hate That'❖
'Gone kissing'❖'Tired of screwing? Try riveting'❖'Don't Worry,
It'll Only Seem Kinky the First Time'

THE WORD ON SEXY CLOTHES

❖*Endytophiliacs keep their clothes on when they have sex.*

❖*The words 'trousers' and 'pants' were considered obscenities in 19th century England and replaced with 'inexpressibles' and 'a pair of dittoes' instead.*

❖*Cosplay is a term for dressing up as Japanese anime characters. It can be enjoyed in specialist 'image clubs'.*

❖*Furring is the latest UK craze in furtive erotic rendezvous, where people dress in animal costumes, meet in woods and have sex.*

Uniforms and high heels

Sex experts have found that dressing up often involves power-playing roles and styles that enhance or show off the body without the need to be naked. Sometimes it keeps you in touch with the alter-masculine or feminine side. Couples often dress up and use symbolic props to act out fantasies, which can also be a source of confidence. Many don military uniforms or dress as French maids, nurses and firefighters. Typical fetish fabrics are PVC, leather and latex, which possess sensual tactile and figure-hugging qualities. People who favour these materials are called 'rubberists', while they are also associated with dominatrices; 'leather culture' came in in the 1960s with the rise of S&M. Cross-dressing, however, is generally for comfort and is also called transvestism, a term first coined by German sexologist Magnus Hirschfeld.

SHOWTIME

Before there were moving pictures to show people
taking off their clothes, there was always the real thing.

DANCE OF THE SEVEN VEILS

As part of the deal which ended up with the head of John the Baptist
on a platter, King Herod Antipas acceded to his niece Salome's request
that she should dance for his birthday. The shedding of veils was
perhaps the first recorded striptease. In Strauss' opera *Salome*, the
well-known score for this scene is played for about seven minutes and
is accompanied by an erotic dance which often ends in stark nudity. It
has inspired countless strip shows in many much seedier venues since.

Celebrity brothel owner

Well-known Elizabethan luvvies, theatre owner Philip Henslowe and
the most highly acclaimed actor of the day Edward Alleyn became
brothers-in-law and business partners. They were apparently also
renowned as brothel owners.

STRIPTEASE

Star of Minsky's Burlesque in the 30s, American stripper Gypsy Rose
Lee began her career at the age of 15 and became famous not only for
taking off her clothes slowly but for teasing with her wit, which
developed out of her initial shyness at performing. In 1979, a bow-tied
and buff men's troupe called the Chippendales turned the tables and
offered women all around the world a dancing-exhibitionist
extravaganza of muscles, baby oil and audience interaction. Now, they
can also be found on mobile phone features, such as screensavers.

PEEP SHOW

Invented in America by Herman Casler in 1894, the Mutoscope showed moving pictures to one person at a time using the 'flip-book' principle. Some of the reels had a risqué theme, the most popular being What the Butler Saw machines, and the idea of peeking through a keyhole leading to the peep show projector known as the 'pay and spray'. Tissues were provided in booths where men could watch films or live sex shows until the coin-operated timer went off, shutting the viewing slot until more money was paid. It was the first mechanical sexual entertainment.

POLES APART

Following the Tupperware and Avon models but much racier, pole dancing parties became the USA's first big fitness and health craze of the 21st century, giving women the chance to 'refind their inner sex kitten' and burn up calories in a G-string, while ensuring their men no longer needed to go out for erotic entertainment. Pole dancing has become so respectable that Oprah tried it out on her show and some companies encourage 'motorized pole dancing' in their stretch limos.

The Bombshell Ballroom in Vancouver holds a 'Pole Yoga' class when pole-dancing poles 'deepen stretch' for postures and help with spinal alignment. More to the point, exotic purple backlights make your skin appear flawless as you exercise.

♦♦♦

The Tesco website in the UK was forced to remove a pole-dancing kit after being accused of 'destroying children's innocence'.

CENSORSHIP

However much the authorities try to shut it out, sex always finds its way back into the world of entertainment. It might pop up in the form of nudity or suggestion, or just reside in the imagination of the audience. Sometimes, it's even the real thing. And then there's pornography…

UK Obscene Publications Act 1857

This far-reaching law came about because two items of business, one a pornography case and the other a bill to control the sale of poisons, were brought before Lord Chief Justice Campbell at more or less the same time. He decided that porn was a form of poison too.

WINDMILL THEATRE

Owner Mrs Henderson and manager Vivian Van Damm revived the English theatre's flagging popularity with 'Revudeville' in 1932. Based on the Parisian shows at the Folies Bergère, noted for their nudity, the Windmill girls were the first in Britain to perform scenes of a 'naturistic' variety – i.e. semi-naked. To get past the Theatres Act of 1843, which gave the authorities the power to ban plays on the grounds of immorality, and at a time when only married couples saw each other without clothes, the Windmill had to take heed of the Lord Chamberlain's warning: 'If it moves, it's rude.' As the cast of girls and boys danced and sang, the spotlight was dimmed and subtly placed on nude girls who had to remain still and represent tasteful classical figures from paintings or sculpture, using props, such as scarves or fruit, to conceal pubic hair. Artistes were not allowed to smile on stage and they had to have the right foot thrust forward so that nothing could be seen in what was called 'the fork'. The fan dancers were the only nudes who could move as they were constantly covered by their giant feather boas. These laws were only dropped in 1968.

The Hays Code

Sexual representation in 1930s America attracted strong opposition in the form of the Hays Code (also known as the Production Code). These government guidelines, enforced from 1934 to 1967, were intended to restore and retain family values in American motion pictures and to protect the country from, among other things, sexual deviance in its various forms – as the code recognized them:

II. Sex The sanctity of the institution of marriage and the home shall be upheld. Pictures shall not infer that low forms of sex relationship are the accepted or common thing.

❶ Adultery, sometimes necessary plot material, must not be explicitly treated, or justified, or presented attractively.

❷ Scenes of Passion
a. They should not be introduced when not essential to the plot.
b. Excessive and lustful kissing, lustful embraces, suggestive postures and gestures, are not to be shown.
c. In general passion should so be treated that these scenes do not stimulate the lower and baser element.

❸ Seduction or Rape
a. They should never be more than suggested, and only when essential for the plot, and even then never shown by explicit method.
b. They are never the proper subject for comedy.

❹ Sex perversion or any inference to it is forbidden.

❺ White slavery shall not be treated.

❻ Miscegenation (sex relationships between the white and black races) is forbidden.

❼ Sex hygiene and venereal diseases are not subjects for motion pictures.

❽ Scenes of actual child birth, in fact or in silhouette, are never to be presented.

❾ Children's sex organs are never to be exposed.

HUSTLER V FALWELL

When Larry Flint's pioneering magazine of crude humour and nude women decided to print a parody of a Campari ad featuring fundamentalist minister Jerry Falwell in an incestuous role with his mother, Falwell sued. A disclaimer at the bottom of the page said, 'Ad parody, not to be taken seriously', but although Falwell lost his libel claim he did win $200,000 for 'emotional distress'. In 1988, the Supreme Court reversed the verdict as the First and 14th Amendments prohibit public figures from receiving damages for emotional distress based on satire.

'Nothing is obscene providing it is done in bad taste.' Russ Meyer

The Motion Picture Association of America (MPAA)

NC-17: Old X rating. 18 and over only.

R: Anyone under 17 must be accompanied by an adult.

This voluntary US film rating system began in 1968. Studios generally won't release and cinemas won't show any title above R.

British Board of Film Classification (BBFC)

18: Old X rating. Films for adults only, to buy, rent or see in a cinema, generally depicting simulated sex for 'sexual arousal or stimulation'.

R18: Films for adults only, with real sex for 'sexual arousal or stimulation' and 'explicit works of consenting sex between adults'. Can only be shown in 'specially licensed cinemas, or supplied only in licensed sex shops'.

Office of Film and Literature Classification

R18+: People under 18 cannot rent or exhibit these films.

X18+: People under 18 cannot exhibit, buy or rent these films.

The Australian ratings system was transformed into its current colour-coded format in 2005. Individual states and territories can make further rulings.

Unrated

The now lost *Damaged Goods* (US 1914, UK 1919) was made as a sex education film. On re-release, in 1915, it was a box office smash. It was unrated, but its sensational content about a soldier who catches an STD from a prostitute proved as entertaining as it was instructive.

BANNED

Director Sam Peckinpah's *Straw Dogs* (1971) was banned in the UK due to its brutality and rape scenes. Later recognized as an illustration of man's capabilities when pushed to the edge, rather than a celebration of violence, it was re-released in 2002. In *Crash* (1996), a scientist and an accident victim become obsessed with sex and car collisions. David Cronenberg's 'auto'-erotic film was banned by Westminster Council in the UK, despite winning the *Palme d'Or* at Cannes. ALSO BANNED: ✦ India: *Kama Sutra: A Tale of Love* (1996) ✦ Iran/Iraq/Kuwait/Malaysia: *The 40-Year-Old Virgin* (2005) ✦Malaysia: *Showgirls* (1995) ✦ China: *Brokeback Mountain* (2006) ✦ Oman: *Basic Instinct 2* (2006)

X-Rated

Midnight Cowboy (1969) is the first and only X-rated film to receive the Oscar for Best Film. ❖ In the award-winning and Academy-nominated *Last Tango in Paris* (1973), director Bernardo Bertolucci's fantasies about sex with a stranger formed the basis of his film, which was banned by the Church, while an anal sex scene saw the director and leading cast members arrested. Marlon Brando's unplanned scene caused a scandal in Italy and was as much of a surprise to his leading lady Maria Schneider. ❖ Along with fellow nominee *A Clockwork Orange* (1971), all three X-rated films were later re-released as 'R' – not the X rating's original role. ❖ Russ Meyer's Beyond the *Valley of the Dolls* was contracted as an R-rated sequel, but the finished product earned its X after some major changes.

DIY

*'Don't knock masturbation, it's sex
with someone I love.'* Woody Allen

Until the 1960s, masturbation was considered a sin by many experts, including doctors, educators and members of the Church. It is now accepted that masturbation does not cause blindness, madness, STDs, sterility or pregnancy, and is widely recognized as something most men and women do which may or may not be why there are so many different terms for it, including:

Airing the orchid ♦ *fishing for the mackerel* ♦ *sanding the banister* ♦ *jacking off* ♦ *jerking off* ♦ *whacking off* ♦ *shooting off* ♦ *friggin' your riggin'* ♦ *pulling your pud* ♦ *bashing the bishop* ♦ *firing your peter* ♦ *milking the mouse* ♦ *whipping your turkey* ♦ *charming the snake* ♦ *making the rooster crow* ♦ *peeling the banana* ♦ *juicing the plum* ♦ *tootling your flute* ♦ *bopping the baloney* ♦ *milking your doodle* ♦ *playing pocket pool* ♦ *spanking Elvis*

Commonly used accessories, not all of them advisable, include vacuum cleaner attachments, dolls, vibrators, lubricants and pornography ❖ Methods include the rubdown, waterfall, old reliable, not quite so reliable, belly-scratch, squeeze, autofellation and autocunnilingus ❖ Jack clubs are men-only places, where just manual contact is permitted, often in temporary settings ❖ Jack and Jill events tend to be one-off parties or benefits ❖ Australian research shows masturbating regularly prevents prostate cancer in men ❖ The penalty for masturbation in Indonesia is decapitation ❖ Masturbilia are items to remind someone of the person or thing they are fantasizing about during masturbation.

'If you don't have a good partner, you'd better have a good hand.'
Woody Allen

Self-gratification vs self-abuse

The Egyptians worshipped Atum the sun god as creator of the first people via masturbation, while the Sumerians wrote of Mesopotamian god Enki filling the Tigris with his sperm; in ancient Greece, women regularly used leather and wooden dildos. **Reputedly, Diogenes, the itinerant philosopher, used to masturbate in front of crowds to demonstrate his doctrine of self-sufficiency.** St Augustine of Hippo, of the early Christian church, said that contraceptive sexual activity was a sin worse than rape or incest. **In the Bible, the story of Onan was taken to be anti-masturbatory and by the 18th century the idea that masturbation was harmful came to light via sources such as the writings of Rousseau and the quack pamphlet *Onania* in 1712.** Deterrents, such as potions, metal penis cages and hobbles to keep girls' legs together, were available in the mid-19th century. **Dr John Harvey Kellogg believed his patented breakfast cereal doubled as an antidote to the sins of the flesh, while the father of scouting Lord Baden-Powell spoke of boys going insane from the 'beastliness'.** Sigmund Freud wrote of benefits and disorders, but by the mid-20th century, researchers began to set minds at rest. **In 1948, Alfred Kinsey's 15-year study promoted masturbation as a normal practice, with results showing that 92–97 per cent of men and 62 per cent of women indulged.** Some religious institutions still refute the modern view and recent research shows many men and women still feel guilty and find it hard to talk about it. However, National Masturbation Month in May has been celebrated for more than a decade.

Sleep sex

In June 2007, *Sleep* journal published a report from leading researchers on 'sleep sex'. Carlos Schenck MD of the University of Minnesota and his colleagues found cases of serious injuries caused by unconscious masturbation. This is a condition afflicting both men and women.

FIRST LADIES OF SEX

There ain't nothing like a madame. Claiming to provide
an honest, safe and popular business environment away
from the dangers on the streets, these women are
just helping along what comes naturally.

FRENCH CONNECTIONS

Fernande Grudet, aka the notorious Madame Claude, ran a thriving
high-class call-girl empire whose tentacles stretched from Paris to the
Middle East and Los Angeles in the 1960s and 1970s and which was
allegedly protected, and used, by politicians, the police and VIPs as if it
were a state service. She handpicked her girls, taught them escort
etiquette, chose their lingerie and frocks and educated them in culture,
before turning them loose on appropriate clients, many of whom they
later married. She was convicted of tax evasion and served a four-month
jail sentence in 1986, the same year her memoirs were published.
There is now a restaurant called Madame Claude in Jersey City.

That's their business

Known as 'La Madame Claude Britannique', Scottish 'date sales'
businesswoman Margaret McDonald went from convent school girl to
highly successful international madame running one of the biggest
prostitution rings in Europe, for which she was jailed in 2003. At her
peak, she had 450 young women plus a handful of male escorts listed
on her laptop. Clients paid up to £650 an hour for sex, of which her
cut was 40 per cent, and while the escorts could enjoy jet-setting
around the world with wealthy businessmen and celebrities,
McDonald claimed sex was never paid for and, if it was, then that was
purely between the date and the client.

CYNTHIA PAYNE

Bognor Regis-born Brit Cynthia, who has had two movies made about her colourful life and career – *Personal Services* and *Wish You Were Here* – found fame when she was convicted in 1978 of running 'the biggest disorderly house in history'. She served six months in jail. Her services included parties at which 'luncheon vouchers' were distributed, entitling guests to food, drink and sex with a prostitute. During the wrap party for *Personal Services*, the police raided her house again, leading to further tabloid tales and scandals. This prompted her to stand for Parliament (unsuccessfully) under the banner of the Payne and Pleasure Party, in 1988 and 1992, which campaigned to change Britain's sex laws. Cynthia is now a successful after-dinner speaker.

'If men want sex they'll find it.' Cynthia Payne

HEIDI FLEISS

Known as the Hollywood Madame, Fleiss's career hit the headlines in 1993 when a police sting operation blew the cover on her high-class services, which apparently attracted numerous wealthy and famous clients. During her trial for pandering [providing prostitutes] and tax

evasion, Heidi refused to name any of her high-profile customers, although actor Charlie Sheen revealed he had been one. She was convicted and served 21 months in prison. In 2003 Heidi was hired to be the public face of the Daily Planet in Melbourne, Australia's first brothel to be listed on the stock exchange. In recent times she has applied to open a brothel – Stud Farm – in Nevada, in which male prostitutes will cater for female-only clients.

LOVERS AND LOTHARIOS

'I used to go missing a lot...
Miss Canada, Miss United Kingdom, Miss World.' George Best

'THE STUFF THAT DREAMS ARE MADE OF'

From a conservative background, Hugh Hefner began his lifetime of loving the ladies at 16 when he first fell in love working in a local cinema. He founded *Playboy* magazine in 1953, pioneering a publication that celebrated the 'male-female connection', combining sophisticated articles with sexy pictures of beautiful naked women, which sold up to seven million copies a month. His editorship earned him industry acknowledgement and the bunny logo is recognizable the world over. After his first marriage of 10 years and then 30 years as a bachelor, his second in 1989 was to Playmate of that year Kimberley Conrad. Now separated, she lives next door to his erotic landmark Playboy Mansion in LA, famous for its pool parties, Playmate residents and the ultimate playboy lifestyle. Apparently, tickets for the parties sell for about $2,000 online. In 1998, he marked his return to the single life with the Midsummer Night's Dream lingerie party. Guests at the mansion have included Jack Nicholson, George Clooney, Cameron Diaz and Paris Hilton, while Samantha and the girls were thrown out in an episode of *Sex and the City*. He celebrated his 75th birthday with a pyjama and lingerie party in 2001 and the magazine's 50th anniversary in 2003. Known to have several willing girlfriends at a time, Hef made *The Girls Next Door*, a 2005 television show about his life with Holly Madison, Bridget Marquardt and Kendra Wilkinson. Noted for his trademark silk pyjamas and being a living ad for Viagra, he has been immortalized in a videogame and a new movie biopic.

'Every relationship I've been in, I've overwhelmed the girl.
They just can't handle all the love.' Justin Timberlake

JFK, love god

Although his wife Jackie is reported to have said the charismatic 35th president was too quick in the sack, Angie Dickinson said her time with him was the 'best 20 seconds of my life'. Tales of his sexual exploits include the Secret Service delivering prostitutes to the White House. Other alleged mistresses include Hollywood siren Marilyn Monroe, whose saucy rendition of 'Happy Birthday' in a tight, flesh-coloured dress at the bash for the president's 44th added fuel to the fire; Judith Campbell Exner, who sensationally claimed in her 1977 biography that she was a go-between for JFK and mafia boss Sam Giancana; as well as stripper Blaze Starr and movie stars Audrey Hepburn, Marlene Dietrich and Kim Novak to name but really a few. His appetite for sex has been accounted for as a side-effect from treatment for Addison's Disease, a condition of the adrenal gland leading to hormone deficiency.

GIACOMO CASANOVA, THE GREAT WOMANIZER

The Venice-born 18th century adventurer had a lusty career that took him all over Europe and which was funded by generous patrons, gambling and entrepreneurial endeavour. His autobiography *Histoire De Ma Vie (Story Of My Life)* revealed that he lost his virginity aged 16 to two sisters. He went on to take some 200 lovers, enduring imprisonment and banishment, bankruptcy and numerous scandals. He both swindled and was swindled by several lovers. He possibly had an affair with his own daughter – the child of one of his mistresses – then once the relationship was known to him, carried on a ménage à trois with both mother and daughter.

'Hell, if I'd jumped on all the dames I'm supposed to have jumped on, I'd have had no time to go fishing.' Clark Gable

MISTRESSES

*'Women with pasts interest men because men
hope that history will repeat itself.'* Mae West

Whatever Lola Wants...

Lola Montez was renowned for getting, inspiring the above phrase. The 19th-century, Irish-born Eliza Gilbert eloped with Lieutenant Thomas James at 16. She was a mediocre actress with the reputation for being a 'liberated' woman who traded on her beauty. After taking on the role of a 'Spanish' dancer, she performed around Europe in the 1840s, achieving fame for her wild Spider Dance, which involved lifting her petticoats. She is believed to have had a number of affairs, her partners including writer Alexandre Dumas, composer Franz Liszt and, after performing in Munich, Ludwig I of Bavaria. When he publicly inquired if her bosom was real, she tore her dress open to reveal the proof. He later honoured her with the title of Countess. Following a revolt, she left and married journalist Patrick Hull in California where she received little acclaim and much ridicule for her exotic dancing. In a last-ditch tour of Australia, she caused uproar as apparently she wasn't wearing any underwear.

LILLIE LANGTRY

The twice-married Victorian-Edwardian-era social beauty and actress's most famous lover may have been the Prince of Wales – later Edward VII – but she could also name one or two other notables among her conquests. Edward himself is said to have lost interest in her when she got drunk at a party and slipped on an ice cube; his introduction of her to Prince Louis of Battenberg (father of Lord Louis Mountbatten) was supposedly in order to offload her. She apparently bore his child, a daughter, in 1881. Other lovers included Robert Peel and wealthy racehorse-owner George Baird.

LOUISE BROOKS

Hollywood silent movie star Louise Brooks is famed for her sexual power over men on and off screen. As a rare sexually liberated woman, her philosophy was not generally well received at the time and she was saddled with a bad reputation. Her European films, which include *Pandora's Box* (1929) and the heated tale of *Lulu*, who whores herself for pleasure, has a lesbian encounter and ends up in the hands of Jack the Ripper, feature explicit adult themes, heavily censored. Ironically, at one point her own life followed a similar pattern. When she returned to the USA and failed to regain stardom, she ended up working as a high-class call girl. Apparently, as an elderly woman, she told theatre critic and lover Kenneth Tynan she could still ejaculate across a room.

'The Protestant Whore'

It is thought that Nell Gwyn may have been a child prostitute as well as an oyster-seller. Working in brothels she is said to have been a mistress to several men, but only one at a time. In those days, the word 'whore' related to kept women and adulteresses. When a new theatre was built on Drury Lane, she took on a new career selling fruit and confectionery at the King's Theatre. Then, as a comic actress, she had relationships with reputed artists of the day. She became involved with the king via the Duke of Buckingham who wanted to get closer to the monarch himself, but Nell asked for too much money, leaving the way clear for her friend Moll to be royal mistress. Allegedly, she slipped Moll a dose of powerful laxative before she was due at the king's chambers. The affair with the king is believed to have started in the theatre when he flirted with Nell, and when he invited her out afterwards – with her date – she ended up paying the bill. Although not an official mistress of the Merry Monarch, 'Pretty, witty Nell' Gwyn was a favoured lover of Charles II and stayed with him until his death. He was also the father of her two sons – two of several offspring by his mistresses.

SEX ON TV

GLOBAL ROUND-UP

✻ *Veline* are 'young television assistants who exhibit themselves in scanty clothing during a transmission', and are a staple of Italian television shows. Italian TV also features quiz phone-ins where 'housewives', masked to protect their identity, take off an item of clothing every time contestants correctly answer a question. ✻ One of the most popular shows on Paradise TV (Japan) is *Watashi, Shojo Soshitsu Shimasu (I Will Lose My Virginity)*, where viewers vote for the initiate of their choice and then watch her being deflowered live by an actor, followed by a documentary about her life. *Manko News* is the station's naked news programme. The word *manko* in Japanese is a derogatory term for the vagina, but it is also the name of a tidal wetland area in Okinawa, so they cleverly show pictures of the latter to beat the censor. Genitalia cannot be shown on Japanese TV. ✻ Danwei TV in China make *Sexy in Beijing*, a lavish production inspired by *Sex and the City*. ✻ Large female buttocks are big on Brazilian TV and feature prominently in close-up at peak times. *Popozuda* is Brazilian patois for 'big-buttock woman'.

Stay tuned for more sex

In 2001, a study by the Kaiser Family Foundation found that sexual themes appeared in more than two-thirds of American TV, with 56 per cent in the 1997–1998 season rising to 68 per cent in 1999–2000. In 2005, the study revealed sex scenes had nearly doubled since 1998. ● *Sex and the City* has been broadcast in more than 50 countries worldwide, including Singapore where it was banned until July 2004. *The Simpsons* sent it up by calling it *Nookie in New York, with Marge's sister* describing it as 'a show about four straight women who act like gay men.'

TWO IN A BED

❖ *It is a myth that Fred and Wilma Flintstone were the first couple to be shown in bed together on American TV. The first husband and wife to be televised in bed were the stars of* Mary Kay and Johnny *in 1947, but no footage remains of their antics.*

❖ *The Hays Code of the 1930s reared its ugly head in the 1960s when Barbara Eden* (I Dream of Jeannie), *Sally Field* (Gidget) *and Dawn Wells* (Gilligan's Island) *were forced to cover their navels.*

❖ *Lucille Ball was the first television actress allowed to carry on filming – her comedy series* I Love Lucy, *with on and off-screen husband Desi Arnaz – while she was pregnant, bringing the real-life scenario into the storyline of the show.*

Back after these messages...

Research in 2002 revealed that scenes of a sexual nature can affect the memory. The study by psychologists at Iowa State University involved 324 adults aged 18 to 54 watching programmes with mainstream adverts. They were questioned afterwards and also a day later. Participants who had watched shows with no sexual content had better recall of the commercials than those subjected to sexually graphic content.

CONTACT MUSIC UK'S TOP FIVE SEXIEST FEMALE TV STARS OF ALL TIME

1 Eva Longoria *Desperate Housewives* **2** Jennifer Aniston *Friends*
3 Kim Cattrall *Sex and the City* **4** Pamela Anderson *Baywatch*
5 Sarah Michelle Gellar *Buffy the Vampire Slayer*

TV GUIDE'S TOP FIVE SEXIEST MALE STARS

1 Patrick Dempsey *Grey's Anatomy* **2** Sendhil Ramamurthy *Heroes*
3 James Tupper *Men In Trees* **4** Josh Holloway *Lost* **5** Taylor Kitsch
Friday Night Lights

THE LOVE LIBRARY

The Bloomsbury Group

This was an informal collective of early 20th century writers and artists united by their rejection of the morality and thinking of the Victorian and Edwardian eras. Members experimented with open marriages and many had affairs with people of both sexes. Notable adherents of the group, which ended by the start of WWII, include Virginia Woolf, Vita Sackville-West, EM Forster, Roger Fry and Lytton Strachey.

KAMA SUTRA

These ancient Indian texts by philosopher Mallanaga Vatsyayana are actually mostly about love. A small section deals with sexual behaviour and positions, but rather than being a sex manual as is often thought, the general theme is caring and etiquette, including cooking and calligraphy. The work focuses on partnerships rather than the individual. It promotes mutual sexual appreciation and pleasure as something to be respected rather than be ashamed of.

The Autobiography of a Flea is an anonymously written Victorian erotic novel of 1901. The unknown Flea tells the tale of Bella, innocent and curious, and her leap into the realms of lust, first with Charlie and then with Father Ambrose. It was made into a porno film in 1976.

'Here's how men think: sex, work, food, sports and lastly, begrudgingly relationships. And here's how women think: relationships, relationships, relationships, work, sex, shopping, weight, food.' Carrie Fisher, *Postcards From The Edge*, 1987

Miss Manners' Guide to Excruciatingly Correct Behavior

Miss Manners, aka author Judith Martin, has written an advice column since 1978. Her 'heavy etiquette theory' comes through in wit and serious analysis. The book includes such gems as offering toiletries to a one-night stand and how to get out of scrapes such as calling a lover by another's name.

FANNY HILL (1748 AND 1749)

Published in two parts, the most famous, and apparently the first, erotic novel is a classic rags-to-riches story of an innocent girl who ends up in a brothel where she falls in love with one of the clients. But the riches fall short and she ends up having sex with a number of men to make a living. Author John Cleland wrote it while serving time in a debtors' prison in London. Cleland and his publisher were arrested for producing obscene material and 'corrupting the King's subjects'. It was also banned in the US. In 1963, it was published as *John Cleland's Memoirs of a Woman of Pleasure* and banned again.

'You shall haue euery sawcy boy... to catch vp a woman & marie her... So he haue his pretie pussie to huggle withall, it forceth not.'
Philip Stubbes, *The Anatomie of Abuses*, 1583

Apparently the longest sex book title is *MULIEBRIA Historico-Medica, hoc est Partium Genitalium Muliebrium Consideratio Physico-Medico-Forensis, qua Pudendi Muliebris Partes tam externae, quam internae, scilicet Uterus cum Ipsi Annexis Ovariis et Tubis Fallopianis, nec non Varia de Clitoride et Tribadismo de Hymen et Nymphotomania seu Feminarum Circumsisione et Castratione selectis et curiosis observationibus traduntur* AD Martino Schurigio, Physico Dresdensi (MDCCXXIX) by Schurig. *Muliebria* translates as the female genital organs.

Steamy reading

'While we have sex in the mind, we truly have none in the body.' DH Lawrence, *Leave Sex Alone*, 1929

Most PC book of 2006

And Tango Makes Three by Justin Richardson and Peter Parnell. The award-winning book is about Roy and Sid, a same-sex couple who hatch and raise a chick and become a family.

BANNED FOR SEXUAL THEMES

➼*Catcher in the Rye*, JD SALINGER – in various US schools and libraries ➼*Flower for Algernon*, DANIEL KEYES – school boards including British Columbia and Canada ➼*Lady Chatterley's Lover*, DH LAWRENCE – US and UK temporarily. Australia ➼*Lolita*, VLADIMIR NABOKOV – Iran and Saudi Arabia ➼*Ulysses*, JAMES JOYCE – US temporarily

PLAYBOY'S LIST OF SEXIEST NOVELS EVER (TOP 20)

❶ *Memoirs of a Woman of Pleasure*, John Cleland ❷ *Lady Chatterley's Lover*, DH Lawrence ❸ *Tropic of Cancer*, Henry Miller ❹ *The Story of O*, Pauline Reage ❺ *Crash*, JG Ballard ❻ *Interview with the Vampire*, Anne Rice ❼ *Portnoy's Complaint*, Philip Roth ❽ *The Magus*, John Fowles ❾ *The Wind-Up Bird Chronicle*, Haruki Murakami ❿ *Endless Love*, Scott Spencer ⓫ *Lolita*, Vladimir Nabokov ⓬ *Carrie's Story*, Molly Weatherfield ⓭ *Fear of Flying*, Erica Jong ⓮ *Peyton Place*, Grace Metalious ⓯ *Story of the Eye*, Georges Bataille ⓰ *The End of Alice*, AM Homes ⓱ *Vox*, Nicholson Baker ⓲ *Rapture,* Susan Minot ⓳ *Singular Pleasures*, Harry Mathews ⓴ *In The Cut*, Susanna Moore

'… I saw, with wonder and surprise, what?
not the play-thing of a boy, not the weapon of a man,
but a maypole of so enormous a standard, that had proportions been
observ'd, it must have belong'd to a young giant.' **From *Fanny Hill***

Rules For Writing Real Classy Sex Scenes

Never compare a woman's nipples to: A) Cherries B) Cherry pits C) Pencil erasers D) Frankenstein's bolts ✴ *Never, ever use the words 'penis' or 'vagina'* ✴ *Resist the temptation to use genital euphemisms (unless you are trying to be funny)* ✴ *No:* tunnel of love, candy shop, secret garden, pleasure gate, bearded clam ✴ *Equally no:* mule, flesh kabob, magic wand, shaft of manhood ✴ *Don't forget the foreplay* - The lead-in is often better than the actual humping part. Tease the reader a little ✴ *Real people do not talk in porn clichés* - They do not say: 'Give it to me, big boy.' Most of the time, real people say all kinds of weird, funny things during sex, such as 'I've got a cramp in my foot' ✴ *It is okay to get aroused by your own sex scenes* - in fact, it's pretty much required Source: sbalmond@earthlink.net

THE HITE REPORT

Sexual satisfaction was a key part of the sexual revolution in the 1960s, with pleasure as the main aim. People were talking more openly about sex and according to sex researcher Shere Hite, the time had come to focus on the female orgasm. She showed many women what they had been missing. Using revelations in her anonymous questionnaires from more than 30,000 women aged between 14 and 78, her book *The Hite Report: A Nationwide Study of Female Sexuality* (1976/2004) educated women about sex and sexuality. Hite's findings revealed 70 per cent of women who couldn't achieve orgasm through sexual intercourse were able to by other means, clitoral stimulation and masturbation, and this knowledge should now be shared.

'But Gosh! I've never seen such a fleece between a woman's legs in my life. Darn me if she wouldn't have to be sheared before man could get into her,' said a 'passer-by' on the view of Miss Dean in erotic classic *The Memoirs of Dolly Morton*, 1899

SEX AFTER MARRIAGE

Monogamous relationships may appear to be a relatively modern idea, but anthropologists suggest couples were feeling the urge and getting together on a long-term basis many years ago.

➤ In ancient Rome, marriage was merely a household arrangement, while sex was a guilt-free pleasure. It was normal to attend orgies, prostitutes and courtesans were respected and monogamy was not.

➤ When women in Cali, Colombia, have sex for the first time with their husband, their mother must also be present.

➤ In the Middle Ages, sexual incompetence was considered grounds for divorce – but only if it could be demonstrated in front of a court of law.

➤ According to a survey, American private detectives found white married people were more likely to cheat than other racial groups.

➤ In medieval France, wives who committed adultery had to chase a chicken through the streets wearing no clothing.

➤ Until 1884, a wife could go to jail in England if she deprived her husband of sex.

➤ Wives in Hong Kong are allowed to kill cheating husbands but only with their bare hands.

➤ King Mongut of Siam – played by Yul Brynner in *The King and I* – died of syphilis, admitting he only loved the first 700 of his 9,000 wives.

➤ John Harvey Kellogg, of corn flake fame, was married for more than 40 years but never had sex or shared a bedroom with his wife.

➤ In India, when Toda women marry, they are also bound to have sex with their husband's brothers.

➤ A 'hot wife' in swinging terms is a married woman who has sex with other men with her husband's consent.

'Marriage is miserable unless you find the right person that is your soulmate – and that takes a lot of looking.' Marvin Gaye

*'Don't you know that a man being rich is like a girl being pretty?
You wouldn't marry a girl just because she's pretty, but my
goodness, doesn't it help?'*

Marilyn Monroe in *Gentlemen Prefer Blondes* (1953)

Honeymoon

The honeymoon comes from ancient Babylonia where the bride's father gave mead to be drunk by the newlyweds for a period of a month (a moon phase). Tales from northern Europe speak of the groom capturing his bride, taking her into hiding and getting her pregnant before her family could find her. Once she was pregnant it would be too late and safe to return to his home. In Victorian times, couples would keep their post-wedding trip a secret, even during their time away, to save themselves from the embarrassment of people knowing they were going to have sex.

WHEN THE HONEYMOON IS OVER

In 2006, apparently almost half – 49 per cent – of divorcing couples in Britain employed private investigators to check up on their spouses' fidelity, compared with 18 per cent in 2005. The figure is made up of 30 per cent women and 19 per cent men. Men brought about 69 per cent of adultery cases, women 31 per cent. According to a Kinsey Institute survey, 20 to 25 per cent of men are unfaithful at least once during their marriages, as opposed to 10 to 15 per cent of women. Infidelity is cited as grounds for divorce in more than 150 cultures around the world. A study by the London School of Hygiene and Tropical Medicine revealed that men and women in Britain were more adulterous than the Italians or French.

'Men marry because they are tired, women because they are curious;
both are disappointed.' Oscar Wilde

Nena and George O'Neill's bestseller *Open Marriage* (1972) introduced just that concept to 1970s America, in order to benefit marriage by freeing it from old-fashioned rules, but they did not necessarily recommend additional sexual partners.

THE SEXPERTS

The popular book *A Marriage Manual* (1935) by Hannah and Abraham Stone offered couples advice and information on sexuality in marriage and they also set up America's first marriage guidance service. Their studies found:

❶ *76 per cent of women had a 'normal sexual attitude'* **❷** *20 per cent of women were not interested in sex* **❸** *4 per cent of women did not enjoy sex* **❹** *85 per cent of couples had sex two to three times a week* **❺** *4 per cent had sex on a daily basis.*

In 2006, a Christian couple from south Wales launched a website celebrating sex inside marriage after visiting a sex shop and discovering the high prices. The site offers advice and sex, focusing on the positive side of sex minus the sleaze and with support from church leaders.

'Bachelors know more about women than married men;
if they didn't, they'd be married too.' Henry Louis Mencken

✳

'I know nothing about sex because I was always
married.' Zsa Zsa Gabor

'Sex is always tempting, but always with my husband.'
Kate Hudson, actress, toes the marital line

■ **Monogamy** is when one husband has one wife.

■ **Polygamy** is split into two: **Polygyny**, where one husband has two or more wives. According to studies, this is the most desired form of marriage in three-quarters of the world, but only practised by societies and religions such as the Chinese and Mormons. Polyandry is where one wife has two or more husbands, appealing to only one per cent of the world and practised among societies including Eskimo and Himalayan. **Polyamory** from the Greek *poly* for many and Latin *amor* for love. This is a consensual relationship with more than one partner at the same time, where all parties are equal in love and sex.

An ABC News Primetime Live survey on sex in 2004 revealed 61 per cent of Americans had no problem with premarital sex; divorced or separated men were twice as likely to have cheated; faking orgasms was high among wives who had cheated or were unhappy with their sex life; while 51 per cent of couples discussed their fantasies, which helped towards a happy marriage; and monogamy rules.

'Opportunity knocks for every man, but you have to give a woman a ring.' Mae West

Ancient Egyptians believed the vein of love
ran straight from the ring finger, fourth on the left hand,
to the heart.

♦♦♦

These days, life is perhaps less romantic and 35 per cent of
those who use personal ads for dating are married.

THE NAKED TRUTH

'What spirit is so empty and blind that it cannot recognize the fact that the foot is more noble than the shoe, and skin more beautiful than the garment with which it is clothed?' Michelangelo

The naked body is only natural, but convention still directs most of us to cover up most of the time.

AS NATURE INTENDED

❖ *In many cultures, nakedness is not seen as a taboo* ❖ *In Africa, a piece of string around the waist is the sole covering for some male hunters* ❖ *Only without his natural pod penis cover, which gives the impression of an erection, would a man be in an embarrassing state of undress in some tribes of New Guinea* ❖ *In southern California, the Chumash Native American men were generally naked and the women topless* ❖ *Tribes of the Amazon Basin were usually nude bar a foreskin clamp* ❖ *In some parts of Africa, the sexiest parts of women's bodies are the neck and lips, which they stretch and adorn with jewellery* ❖ *Members of a cargo cult in Vanuatu, South Pacific, began to worship Prince Philip after he and the Queen visited in the 1970s. In a bid to lure him back, they sent him a namba, or penis sheath, via the British High Commission. This is traditionally the tribesmen's only item of clothing.* ❖ *For more than 1,000 years, Japanese men have celebrated their manhood by stripping off at the Kounoniya annual Nude Festival*

◆Topfreedom is a movement promoting women's right to go topless in the same situations as men. ◆Starkers Nightclub in London has a strict undress code where nudity is safe and 'attitude-free' – for the staff and clientele.
◆Strip at Morga Dyffryn beach, Wales, with a nudist camp and beach, was named by *The Sunday Times* as one of the 50 best days out in Britain in 2007

The Naturist Society says that naturism is not a code for sex or lewd behaviour but rather 'a way of living in greater fidelity to nature, with a norm of full nudity in social life, the genitals included, when possible and appropriate. We aim to enhance acceptance and respect for one's self, other persons and the biosphere.' (1997)

SKIN DEEP

In Greek and Roman times, bathing was communal with a focus on cleanliness rather than sex. ✱ *In ancient India, some male spiritual groups participated in a disciplined naked existence, while the Hindu sect of the Sakas celebrated nudity and sex as natural.* ✱ The Jain religion still practises nudity today. ✱ *In the Middle Ages, the Christian Church linked nudity to 'original sin' and cited women as the 'daughters of Eve' so covering up became a necessity.* ✱ The Bonfire of the Vanities in Florence in 1497 witnessed the destruction of 'sinful' Renaissance paintings featuring too much human flesh. ✱ *The prudish Chinese thought that classical Christian paintings of draped saints were pornographic.* ✱ In Victorian England, when nudity was considered indecent, the naughty postcard became extremely popular. Mostly produced in French studios they ranged from artful poses to the downright obscene. ✱ *The first nudist colony in the UK, known as the Moonella Group, was founded in 1924 in Essex, while the first nudist event in the USA took place in woods outside New York in response to an ad by Kurt Barthel, founder of the first official US nudist camp, inviting like-minded people to join him.* ✱ The Sex Party started in British Columbia, Canada, in 2005 calls itself 'the world's first registered political party dedicated exclusively to sex-positive issues', promoting public nudity and a gradual learning of sexual activity.

'Sex is a part of nature. I go along with nature.' Marilyn Monroe

DO BLONDES HAVE MORE FUN?

Are blondes really dumb and dependent on men, and why is this attractive? Are Tinkerbell, Cinderella and Goldilocks good role models, or is it all one big fairy tale? Could blondes actually be dark horses who know exactly how to get what they want?

'I can be smart when it's important, but most men don't like it.'
Marilyn Monroe in *Gentlemen Prefer Blondes* (1953)

Blonde Ambition

The evolution of the blonde, 11,000 years ago, happened during the Ice Age to help gain advantage in sexual selection. At a time when males were scarce, blondes stood out among their predominantly dark European rivals, first creating the idea of blonde appeal in men's minds.

GENTLEMEN NO LONGER PREFER BLONDES

In the West, blonde hair is still regarded as a positive and attractive attribute in women. From the 1950s to the 1980s, research showed a considerable number of blondes were used in ads and magazines, with *Playboy* promoting the sexy blonde and 84 per cent of women believing men preferred blondes. However, the actual percentage was 35.

*'Blonde jokes don't bother me because I know I'm not dumb
and I know I'm not blonde.'* Dolly Parton

In Greek mythology, the most desirable characters and gods were blond, from Helen of Troy to Aphrodite.

♦♦♦

The Romans wore pillaged Nordic plaits as trophies.

BLONDE INTELLIGENCE

● *All top 10 finalists of the 2007 Miss Universe were brunettes.* ● *In AD300, Christians believed the blonde naked Venus represented evil.* ● *In 2007, a survey by Sunsilk and Askmen showed that 85% of men preferred brunettes for intelligence, marriage and sex.* ● *The International Blondes Association was set up by disgruntled blondes in Finland in 1998.* ● *In 360BC, Praxiteles created a statue of a blonde Aphrodite, inspiring women to lighten their hair and the poet Menander to say, 'No chaste woman ought to make her hair yellow.'*

● *Queen Elizabeth I chose blond hair as a symbol of virtue.* ● *According to Jerry Oppenheimer's biography, Paris Hilton's parents are proud of the sex video that made her a star.* ● *Anita Loos, author of* Gentlemen Prefer Blondes *(1925) also wrote the sequel,* But Gentlemen Marry Brunettes *(1928).* ● *A 2006 poll at UK shopping mall Lakeside named Dame Helen Mirren as the sexiest older woman.* ● *Durex named first blond Bond Daniel Craig as the sexiest man in the world, with David Beckham at number seven.*

Dumb blondes

The sexy, fun-loving, promiscuous dumb blonde stereotype was promoted by Hollywood icons, such as Jean Harlow and Marilyn Monroe. In *Gentlemen Prefer Blondes* (1953), while both blonde and brunette are sexy, Monroe is the vacuous gold-digger, and Jane Russell is sharp and witty, but the real message is female sexual power. The list of headlining blondes goes on and on, including Mae West, Bridget Bardot, Jayne Mansfield, Grace Kelly, Kim Novak, Diana Dors, Debbie Reynolds, Margaret Thatcher, Lady Diana, Sharon Stone and Scarlett Johansson. Blond men have often been portrayed as weak or villainous, leaving the tall, dark and handsome to take the romantic lead, with the exception of men and women's men Steve McQueen, Paul Newman and Robert Redford, and now the likes of David Beckham, Daniel Craig and Brad Pitt, who are giving the tall, dark and handsome a run for their money.

SEX TOMORROW

'I can remember when the air was clean and the sex was dirty.'
George Burns 1896–1996

Peering through a telescope into the future, it appears that, thanks to science, our sex lives are about to take off as never before. We will take advantage of advances in surgical techniques to acquire perfect bodies, make use of 'neuromacrosensing' which sends in microscopic 'nanobots' to caress sensitive areas with pinpoint accuracy (producing unprecedented orgasms) and, in the coming world of virtual reality, we'll be able to 'hold orgies on the moon of Jupiter, on lambskin rugs, with cherubim as an attentive audience' – well, that's according to James Hughes (see p.183). Now that scientists are likely to take over the messy business of procreation, sex will be purely for pleasure. Leaving aside one worrying question – if we no longer need our sex organs for procreation, will evolution rid us of them? – futurologists are predicting drugs which sort out every kind of sexual malfunction and switch libido on and off like a light, 'teledildos' operated by computer for those who like to be probed from afar and underwear packed with sensors for couples bored with the limitations of current video games. In the future, everybody will have their own 'bio-tailors', godlike doctors who can give or take away breasts, sort you out with a penile implant or two and who will run you up a bespoke sex life in exchange for a large bag of money. The possibilities are endless.

Living dolls

In 2006, Henrik Christensen of the European Research Network told *The Sunday Times*, 'People are going to be having sex with robots within five years.' Sex dolls have been around for hundreds of years and *dames de voyage*, lifesize females made of cloth, were particularly popular aboard ships. These days cheap vinyl blow-ups are run of the mill, but if you want the Rolls-Royce of 'gentlemen's companions', then Abyss Creations' 'realdolls' are a snip at $6,499. With nine heads to choose from, five porn-standard body styles and three working orifices supplied as standard, you can create your own idealized version of womanhood with perfect silicone skin, 'breasts that can stand 400 per cent elongation without tearing' and 'articulated skeletons which allow for anatomically correct positioning'. Other models include the Male as well as the She-Male, and Abyss are looking to supply electronic and animatronic versions in the very near future. In the meantime, even if a realdoll can't do the hoovering, you're guaranteed she won't talk back or run up a huge bill on your credit card.

'Today's transgender movement is a roiling, radical critique of the limit of gender roles, with folks living in totally new categories, such as non-op transsexual, TG butch, femme queen, gender-queer, cross-dresser, third gender, drag king or queen and transboy. A person with breasts and a penis may dress and identify as a woman and have a sexual preference for women. In the 21st century all the aspects of sexual dimorphism are up for mix and match to suit our psychological needs and aesthetic preferences. By the 22nd century, when we are facing indefinite lifespans, tweaks to biological gender will become increasingly common, to stay in fashion, to improve your chances in life and love, or just out of curiosity.'

James Hughes, Executive Director, Institute for Ethics and Emerging Technologies

The Future's Not Sexy...

☎ In June 2007. the Carphone Warehouse's Mobile Life study revealed that, if made to choose, the majority of 16- to 24-year-olds would rather give up sex than surrender their mobile phones, while most over-45-year-olds would rather give up sex than their regular cup of coffee or tea.

☎ On the other hand, you never need to be alone in Japan thanks to mobile phones and global positioning systems. If you want a partner, just let a dating service check who's in the vicinity and they will fix you up with an 'offkai', or offline meeting, in next to no time. Some Japanese women own mobiles that keep them tuned in to their ovulation cycle. If the koala bear climbs the tree, the woman's temperature is rising. If the bear is on his way down, conception is much less likely. Mobile phones are set to play a bigger role in our sex lives. Japanese scientists are predicting a 'cell phone that gives you orgasms'.

IT'S GREEN

A number of environmental organizations are encouraging people to save the planet without losing touch with their sex lives. Suggestions to protect the future include:

() *switching from dimming electric lights to burning soy candles*
() *using solar-powered sex toys and encouraging the ban of toxic chemicals*
() *buying products with the least packaging and more organic ingredients, including lubricants, vegan condoms, bamboo sheets and eco lingerie made from hemp but designed to be sexy*

You know you're addicted to web porn when... you tilt your head to the side every time you smile.

SEX TECH

Popular internet-based simulation Second Life is experiencing more and more sexual activity. Cybersex is becoming one of its most popular online activities, with the virtual world playing host to sex clubs for fans of long-distance computer love. Sex is limited to specialist sex zones, where users can begin with chat and description, and then move on to animated sex. Now programmers are taking things forward with specially designed genitals for players and complex 'in-world' sex toys. The fantasy element means control: users decide how sexy they wish to be and how much cyberskin to reveal, what kind of body parts and props they want and what they can do. The idea is to customize personal desires.

FROZEN FAMILY

Professor Carl Djerassi, whose discoveries played a huge part in the development of the Pill, the groundbreaking contraceptive, in the 1960s, making sex without children possible, is now focusing on the next cultural revolution: children without sex. With women spending more time on careers and egg-freezing methods, such as vitrification, advancing all the time, he predicts an increasing number will freeze their eggs for use when the time is right to start a family. With independence, education and financial stability as well as a longer lifespan, women are no longer such dependent beings.

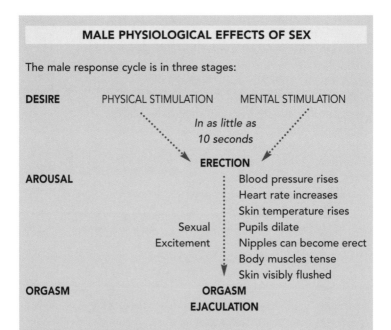

MORE THAN A FEELING

It's a pleasure to make love, but what happens to the body, and do men and women experience the same feelings and effects?

MALE PHYSIOLOGICAL EFFECTS OF SEX

The male response cycle is in three stages:

DESIRE   PHYSICAL STIMULATION   MENTAL STIMULATION

In as little as 10 seconds

ERECTION

AROUSAL

Sexual
Excitement

Blood pressure rises
Heart rate increases
Skin temperature rises
Pupils dilate
Nipples can become erect
Body muscles tense
Skin visibly flushed

ORGASM   **ORGASM**
                     EJACULATION

Orgasm is the release of muscular tension and engorged blood vessels. Semen is expelled in rhythmic contractions, reaching a peak of flow, then a reduction to smaller spurts. Few men experience second and third orgasms.

> *'Men don't fake orgasm –*
> *no man wants to pull a face like that on purpose.'*
> Allan 'Mr Body Language' Pease

FEMALE PHYSIOLOGICAL EFFECTS OF SEX

'I used both hands to hide
My blushing, sweating cheeks. Indeed, I tried.
But oh, what could I do, then, when I found
My bodice splitting of its own accord?'

From *When His Mouth Faced My Mouth*, Amaru, c. AD800,
translated by John Brough

The female response cycle is in three stages of desire, arousal and orgasm:

- ◆ Physical and mental stimulation
- ◆ Vaginal lubrication
- ◆ Vagina lengthens, distends and walls fill with blood
- ◆ Labia is erect
- ◆ Clitoris is erect
- ◆ Breasts swell
- ◆ Nipples become erect
- ◆ Uterus and cervix move forward
- ◆ Heart rate increases
- ◆ Blood pressure rises
- ◆ Skin visibly flushed
- ◆ Vagina changes to resemble a tent shape
- ◆ Vagina exudes secretion

Orgasm produces limb jerking and powerful trembling; the uterus and anus contract; and orgasmic contractions are similar to the male. Some women can experience multiple orgasms.

'Sex can still be great, even without an orgasm.'
Kristin Davis

FEEL THE BENEFIT

❖ The brain cannot distinguish between a sneeze and an orgasm.

❖ As a cardiovascular exercise, sex can help reduce the risk of heart disease.

❖ Sexercise helps weight loss and fitness.

❖ Regular sex helps combat stress and depression.

❖ The after-effects of orgasm provide relaxation and a good night's sleep.

❖ Sex boosts the immune system, warding off colds, and gives relief from joint pain.

❖ Sometimes called 'God's gift to women', the clitoris has no other known function beyond sexual pleasure.

Stay beautiful

♦**Pain relief** A headache is no excuse. Painkilling endorphins and good vibrations are exciting soothers released during orgasm.

♦**Perfect skin** Sex increases the body temperature and gentle sex can help prevent skin problems as sweat cleanses the pores and makes the skin glow. Women produce double the amount of oestrogen, which as well as making skin smooth, keeps hair shiny.

♦**Chemical bond** Known as the love, cuddle and bonding hormone, oxytocin is released from the posterior lobe of the pituitary gland at the base of the brain and encourages touchy-feely contact.

The English word 'penis' comes from Latin and it originally meant the tail of an animal. 'Pene' is Latin for 'inside' and it may have implied the part that goes inside (the vagina). The correct plural is either 'penes' or 'penises'.

♦♦♦

Ithyphallophobia is a fear of seeing, thinking about or having an erect penis.

'The mind can also be an erogenous zone.' Raquel Welch

Cosmopolitan magazine's top five male erogenous zones
❶ Cremaster Muscle ❷ Prostate ❸ Lips
❹ Nipples ❺ Perineum

AskMen.com top ten female erogenous zones
❿ Inner thighs ❾ Behind the knees ❽ Buttocks
❼ Nape of the neck ❻ Ears ❺ Feet
❹ Wrists ❸ Breasts (nipples)
❷ Vagina/clitoris ❶ Lips

'You're a woman of many parts, Pussy.' James Bond, *Goldfinger*

ON THE RIGHT SCENT

Many researchers believe humans give off aphrodisiacal pheromones, scents which affect sexual desire and behaviour, and suggest healthy offspring. In 1996, Swiss scientist Claus Wedekind studied 44 men, who each wore a T-shirt for two days without washing. The unwashed T-shirts were given to a group of women to smell and choose partners. The men with similar immune systems to the women's own were compared with their fathers or brothers; they preferred the men whose immune systems were most different.

'Blake said that the body was the soul's prison unless the five senses are fully developed and open. He considered the senses the "windows of the soul". When sex involves all the senses intensely, it can be like a mystical experience.' Jim Morrison, the Doors

Quickies

✦ 'Dressing' is when a man positions 'the family jewels' to one side of the trousers.

✦ In 2006, Spam-Filter-Review.com found 19 per cent of spam to be of an adult nature.

✦ An 'alley affair' is sex in a deserted public space.

✦ A lucky Pierre is a male three-way.

✦ With the average amount of sex a typical American couple has, it would take them about four years to get through all of the 529 positions of the *Kama Sutra*.

✦ About 500 Americans die each year from asphyxia during sex.

✦ Using a strap-on dildo on a partner is called 'pegging'.

✦ A cuckold was an adulterous woman in medieval times, who made a 'cuckoo' of her husband, just as the female bird would lay eggs in another bird's nest, freeing her from all responsibility.

✦ Baisiexia is sexual arousal from kissing.

✦ An American trombone is a threesome with the woman bending over in the middle.

✦ Dry humping is usually performed on the dance floor, or anywhere it would be inappropriate to get undressed, and means getting as intimate as possible with clothes on.

✦ A 'train' is a line of people waiting to have sex or a line of men each penetrating the man in front.

✦ A booty call is a reliable source of last-minute sex, generally like ordering a pizza. A booty break is time off from sex.

SEX AND THE CIGARETTE

'Love is an exploding cigar we willingly smoke.' Lynda Barry

THE POST-COITAL CIGARETTE

One of the biggest clichés in the packet, the after-sex smoke became popular thanks to the extra rush to the head and a chance to lie back and take in the moment that had just passed. It also looked cool in the movies; the audience didn't always see the sex but they could imagine.

MASS SEX APPEAL

The association of smoking and sex was fired up by Hollywood and the advertising world, with stars like Bogart and Bacall apparently inviting the smoker to share their exotic lifestyles. Ad campaigns in the 19th century had used risqué pictures of scantily clad women and dancers. In the 20th century, however, smokers wanted to identify with their pin-up idols, to acquire some of their sexual charisma. They were duly bombarded with sophisticated advertising that promised men sexual success and women mystery and allure. Stars like Rock Hudson, Greta Garbo, Marlene Dietrich and Lana Turner were used. Artist George Petty, whose famous Petty Girls were usually found in *Esquire*, produced ads for Old Gold in the 1930s: a small bald guy was accompanied by leggy young dream girls, with the message 'For young ideas! Stimulating... but never irritating.' In 1952, Marilyn Monroe appeared on Diplomat Cigarettes in a sexy black lace number; this was actually an overprint on a nude photograph she had posed for in a 1951 calendar, but the effect was equally appealing. Audrey Hepburn, with the must-have sexual fashion accessory, a cigarette holder, dangling from her fingers, epitomized elegance in *Breakfast at Tiffany's* (1961). In 1969, cigarette commercials were banned from TV.

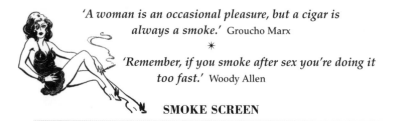

'A woman is an occasional pleasure, but a cigar is always a smoke.' Groucho Marx

*

'Remember, if you smoke after sex you're doing it too fast.' Woody Allen

SMOKE SCREEN

Cigarettes and sex came as a package; a shared cigarette began a relationship or ended a memorable sex session. In *Now Voyager* (19), Bette Davis and Paul Henreid shared cigarettes as a metaphor for sex; in *Chinatown* (1974), Jack Nicholson and Faye Dunaway share a cigarette after sex; in *Grease* (1978), the moment Sandy becomes sexy and finally wins Danny's desire is when she coolly impresses him with her new habit and stubs out a cigarette with her stiletto sandal. *Airplane* (1980) parodies the post-coital cigarette cliché in the scene where Julie Hagerty and Otto the inflatable automatic pilot enjoy a smoke after she has blown him up in a scene made to look like oral sex.

Seductive slogans

❋ 'MORE SMOKING PLEASURE THAN YOU EVER HAD BEFORE... THEY SATISFY!' Chesterfield ❋ 'SLOW DOWN. PLEASURE UP.' 'BLOW SOME IN MY DIRECTION.' Camel ❋ 'I LOVE TO SEE A MAN SMOKE A CIGARILLO' Cigarillos ❋ 'WHY DON'T YOU PICK ME UP AND SMOKE ME SOME TIME?' Muriel Cigars

'Want better sex? Put out that cigarette. Smoking decreases libido.' Quit Smoking Support